MW00527619

In your hands is a powerful and accessible guide to help create a culture marked by health and goodness. Laura Barringer and Scot McKnight do much more than just name the troubling state of many church communities. They offer an extensive set of practices and values to actually live into the tov life God desires for us. I'll be enthusiastically sharing this with many!

RICH VILLODAS, lead pastor, New Life Fellowship, and author of *Good and Beautiful and Kind*

Scot and Laura offer strategically hopeful truth in this book. The mass uncovering of abusive practices, systems, and personalities has brought with it a feeling of paralysis. The problem seems so comprehensive and entrenched that it leaves many of us staggering for any kind of hopeful action. *Pivot* is a good and godly answer to this cynical feeling. Not just a catchy title, *Pivot* is a prophetic invitation to *move*. Move toward healing, move toward the light, move toward being the change that is so needed right now. This is exactly what I pray for—the wisdom and clarity to *move* toward wholeness together. This book is going to help us all.

DANIELLE STRICKLAND, advocate, author, and speaker

If *tov* is the why, *Pivot* is the how. Scot McKnight and Laura Barringer's new book is rich in theology, and it makes the principles of integrity accessible for those who lead and support faith communities that yearn to grow in Christlikeness. An absolute must-read!

STEVE CARTER, pastor and author of *The Thing Beneath the Thing*

Nearly a decade ago, moral failures among church leaders seemed rare and unusual. But in recent years the curtains have been pulled back, exposing what's beneath the surface: toxic church cultures. No longer can church leaders point the finger at other churches; instead, it's time to do the hard work and examine our own communities and discover where toxicity exists, with the hope of being transformed into tov. Scot McKnight and Laura Barringer provide practical tools to help pastors and church leaders develop pathways from toxic cultures to tov. Every church leader and pastor should have a sense of urgency that we are *all* at risk of developing toxic cultures; and that intentionality, hard work, discernment, and prayer are needed more than ever. This book belongs in the hands of leaders in every church in America.

TARA BETH LEACH, pastor and author of *Radiant Church*

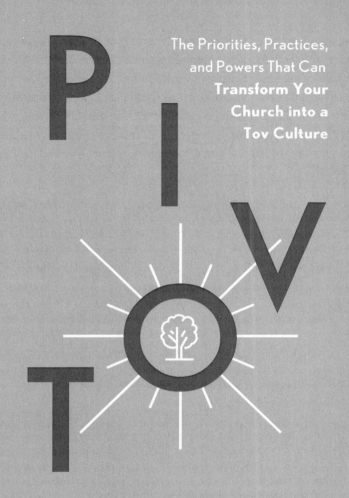

PIVOT

The Priorities, Practices, and Powers That Can **Transform Your Church into a Tov Culture**

SCOT McKNIGHT
LAURA BARRINGER

TYNDALE
elevate™
ask. seek. find.

Visit Tyndale online at tyndale.com.

Tyndale and Tyndale's quill logo are registered trademarks of Tyndale House Ministries. *Tyndale Elevate* and the Tyndale Elevate logo are trademarks of Tyndale House Ministries. Tyndale Elevate is a nonfiction imprint of Tyndale House Publishers, Carol Stream, Illinois.

Pivot: The Priorities, Practices, and Powers That Can Transform Your Church into a Tov Culture

Cover designed by Faceout Studio, Spencer Fuller

For information about special discounts for bulk purchases, please contact Tyndale House Publishers at csresponse@tyndale.com, or call 1-855-277-9400.

Library of Congress Cataloging-in-Publication Data

A catalog record for this book is available from the Library of Congress.

ISBN 978-1-4964-6673-0

Printed in the United States of America

29	28	27	26	25	24	23
7	6	5	4	3	2	1

For the transformers

CONTENTS

FOREWORD BY JOHN ROSENSTEEL *ix*

INTRODUCTION: UNTIL CHRIST IS FORMED IN US *1*

1. Transformation Is Possible, but Not Easy *7*
2. Change Starts with the Soil *19*

PART 1: THREE PIVOTAL PRIORITIES

3. Form Tov Character *35*
4. Practice Tov Power *59*
5. Become a Tov Example *83*

PART 2: THREE PIVOTAL PRACTICES

6. Build a Coalition *101*
7. Take One Step at a Time *121*
8. Create Pockets of Tov *137*

PART 3: THREE PIVOTAL POWERS

9. Nurture Congregational Culture *153*
10. Rely on the Holy Spirit *173*
11. Depend on Grace *187*
    Epilogue: Tov Is Worth It *201*

ACKNOWLEDGMENTS *205*

APPENDIX: THE TOV TOOL *207*

NOTES *217*

ABOUT THE AUTHORS *225*

FOREWORD

BOXER MIKE TYSON FAMOUSLY SAID, "Everybody has a game plan until they get punched in the face."[1] I experienced that reality eight years ago when my family and I moved from a healthy and thriving church in the Midwest to be part of the rebirth of a struggling church in Portland, Oregon. We had a game plan until we didn't. You will read a bit of our story in the pages to come, but suffice it to say, participating in the transformation of a crumbling church has been the most daunting and difficult experience of our lives. Our church almost didn't make it. We almost didn't make it.

Pivot is a sequel of sorts to *A Church Called Tov*—which I encourage you to read if you haven't already. *Tov* found deep resonance with pastors and parishioners who knew something was wrong in their churches but didn't know how to name it. It honestly and lovingly diagnoses what ails and plagues the body of Christ—particularly in the Western world. It calls the church to become a community of goodness that will resist abusive power and champion restorative healing. *Pivot* provides a pathway for that to happen.

Scot and Laura do not write from the cheap seats. They are in the game. They love the church. They offer legitimate critiques, while also providing hopeful solutions. They have both endured deep wounds from the church yet have allowed those wounds to become a catalyst for offering a better way. They speak, pray, and live for a more beautiful church. Their prophetic voice provides lantern light to navigate the gathering darkness. I am deeply grateful for the gift of this book.

The shockwave of 2020 was the great revealer of the American church. It fast-tracked the exposure of blind spots and brokenness that previously were either hidden or ignored. Simmering fault lines erupted. Most pastors I know thought our churches were healthier than they actually were. The lack of Christlikeness on display from many followers of Jesus has been staggering. As we take stock, we must remember that "every system is perfectly designed to get the results it gets."[2] This stark reality has been humbling. It has caused many of us to tear up our playbooks. Returning to pre-COVID status quo does not seem like a viable option. If insanity is "doing the same thing expecting different results," then doubling down on what got us here is insane. We must be done with Whac-A-Mole discipleship. Instead, we need a complete renovation of the heart.

Our churches, and those of us who help lead them, must be committed to deep, restorative, and enduring transformation. The church as the body of Christ is still the hope of the world. There is no plan B. Until Jesus returns, the Kingdom comes to earth-as-it-is-in-heaven primarily through the local church.

Pivot provides invaluable insights that will invigorate and fuel the transformation our churches so desperately need. Don't just read it— ponder it, pray over it, and most important, practice it. *Pivot* is brimming with workable wisdom. Each chapter offers an assortment of tools that will help infuse *tov* into your church's DNA. And don't read it alone. Changing culture is a team sport. Buy copies for others in your community and invite them to join you in the journey of helping your church become an outpost of goodness, beauty, and truth.

As I read *Pivot*, I was bursting with hope and anticipation. I can hardly wait to put it into practice. I was also bummed. If I'd had this book eight years ago, or even three years ago, I may have made fewer mistakes. I may have been a more effective leader. Our church would likely be further along. Simply put, this book will save you from pay-ing some significant "stupid tax."

Sadly, some of my pastor friends have already tapped out. Some have left church altogether. I don't say that with any sense of judg-ment. I get it. About once a week, I am tempted to apply for my dream job stocking shelves at Trader Joe's. But I just can't. Too much is at stake. I've been part of the problem, and by God's grace I long to be part of the solution.

As we slowly make our way out of an apocalyptic season, I am hopeful. Hints of a coming dawn color the horizon. A fresh wind of the Spirit is blowing. A faithful remnant is rising up. More people are praying. More people are walking the talk. More people are hungry for all that is wrong with the world to be made right again. More people are seeking to be part of the *tov* renaissance. I'm guessing you are one of these people. May we together be faithful stewards of our missional moment.

Lest we forget, Scot and Laura remind us that the work of trans-formation is God's job—a work we are invited to join. We have the privilege of being part of the great redemptive story in which (to borrow Tolkien's words) "everything sad [is] going to come untrue."[3] Might God be gathering the scattered and tattered pieces of the church and making something far more glorious than was ever pos-sible before it was broken and lost? Might beauty be emerging from the ashes? I think so, and *Pivot* paints a picture of what that could look like.

As we ponder, pray, and practice this book, here is my prayer:

Father, may we know that we are your beloved and that you chase us with a jealous love that never quits. We grieve with you for your church. Bring her back to life. Restore the years the locusts have eaten. And protect us from evil.

   Come, Lord Jesus. We fix our eyes on you. We are weary and heavy laden. May we not lose heart. Give us rest for our souls. And will you give us new wineskins? Will you give us new wine? Because of you, there is always hope.

Holy Spirit, may we have ears to hear. Move with reviving power in our midst. Raise our dry bones from the grave. May we dance once again as we joyfully celebrate and embody goodness in the land of the living.

To God be the glory. All is grace.

John Rosensteel
New Hope Church, Portland, Oregon

UNTIL CHRIST IS FORMED IN US

SINCE PUBLISHING *A CHURCH CALLED TOV* in October 2020, we have collectively given more than 150 interviews about toxic church cultures and how to form healthy ones that resist abuses of power, followed by countless open and honest conversations about the topic. We have felt encouraged by the numbers of *tov*-seeking folks who desire goodness, transformation, and the healing grace of Christ in their churches, ministries, and nonprofit organizations.

But we still hear far too many stories about serious, ongoing abuses. To those who have written to us, called us, and entrusted us with their stories, we want to affirm that your stories are sacred. We hold them tenderly. We continue to hope and trust for a better way. What you have endured is not God's design for the church; it isn't right, nor is it the way anyone should be treated.

After all we've seen and heard, we still believe it's possible for church cultures to be transformed from toxic to tov. But how? This book seeks to answer that question.

COMMON QUESTIONS

Here are four of the most common questions people have asked us about culture transformation:

1. How can I transform the culture in my church or organization to make it more tov?
2. I believe my workplace is toxic or has unhealthy (hidden) values. How do I initiate change?
3. How do I establish or unleash a culture of goodness in my ministry?
4. I'm not in a position of church leadership. What are some red flags that indicate a toxic culture, and what can I do if I see them?

This book contains the best answers we have found to those questions and others.

We are equipped as teachers, not culture consultants; but during more than a year of rich, Spirit-led conversations with men and women who bravely shared their stories, we sought to learn everything we could about the transformation process. We spoke with gifted transformation agents whom God has used to renovate the culture in their own churches. We read widely about organizational transformation, leadership, and culture shifts. From this mixture, we identified several indispensable practices of organizations that have successfully transformed their internal culture—or are well on their way.

In addition to sharing what we have learned, we also offer a collection of useful assessments, tools, and application exercises designed to help you as you labor in cooperation with God's Spirit to begin transforming your church or organization from toxic to tov.

A HIDDEN POWER

The culture of any organization, including a church, is largely invisible and mostly—sometimes completely—unrecognized. Yet organizational culture is the most powerful force underlying how things operate. Though many of the factors involved are unknown to us, they influence our daily lives.

Edgar Schein wrote a highly influential book on organizational culture, titled *Organizational Culture and Leadership*. It describes the enormous psychological power of culture:

> Culture as a set of basic assumptions defines for us what to pay attention to, what things mean, how to react emotionally to what is going on, and what actions to take in various kinds of situations. . . .
> Culture at this level provides its members with a basic sense of identity and defines the values that provide self-esteem. . . . Cultures tell their members who they are, how to behave toward each other, and how to feel good about themselves. Recognizing these critical functions makes us aware why "changing" culture is so anxiety provoking.[1]

Such enormous psychological power should warn us to become aware of culture and never to underestimate it. We cannot over-emphasize the power of a culture to influence, shape, form, and even transform us.

SHIFT, CHANGE, AND TRANSFORMATION

We chose the word *pivot* as the title of this book to describe our purpose. We envision churches around the globe transforming their congregations by pivoting toward a *tov* culture—a culture of good-ness that resists all patterns of abuse that might creep into their communities. We use the terms *shift*, *change*, and *transformation* to describe modifications in a culture, but they differ significantly in scope.

Shift refers to moving one thing in a culture to another place in that same culture. Think of switching the timing of the Sunday sermon from the final event in the worship service to a middle event. Or moving the church's piano from the right side of the sanctuary to the left side. Shifts leave the culture largely undisturbed (though some people inevitably will be upset).

Change in a culture refers to making a significant adjustment within an existing culture, but without deeply changing the culture itself. Think of a church calling a new pastor, who brings his own approach to preaching, teaching, and leading but generally conforms to existing expectations. Or of a church that decides to change the focus of the Sunday service from an evangelistic event for seekers to a time of worship and Bible exposition for Christians. Similarly, a culture change will occur if church leadership decides to call a director of justice and compassion to pioneer a new ministry. Culture changes are more likely than shifts to disturb parishioners. Changes may also generate a desire for deeper adjustments, which we refer to as *transformation*. But changing a culture doesn't necessarily lead to transformation.

A culture is a delicate ecosystem; it is possible, but difficult, to transform an entire ecosystem. One change, or a few small changes, however good, will not result in transformation. The intricacy of a cultural ecosystem demands respect and requires caution with sweeping changes.

Culture *transformation* refers to a revolution or renovation from one type of organization to another. Think of a talent- or gifts-based church transforming into a character formation culture; or from an attractional, seeker-focused model to a spiritual formation model. To undo one type of culture and transform it into another type of culture takes time, commitment, careful communication, and perseverance. It's much easier to dream about it than to actually do it. But if you're dealing with a toxic culture today, nothing short of transformation will bring about the necessary changes to get your organization to tov.

Not everyone uses these three terms—*shift*, *change*, and *transformation*—the way we do, but it's important to distinguish the various levels. The most distinctive difference between shifts, changes, and transformation is that the first two are top-down and usually driven by a leader's creative vision. Transformation occurs only when ownership and participation happen *comprehensively* throughout the organization. This doesn't mean *everyone*, because some people will inevitably opt out and leave, but it does mean widespread participation and buy-in. In the case of a toxic culture under transformation toward tov, rooting out the toxic elements may lead to substantial turnover or attrition. But it's the only way.

This book explores the major contours of the pivot toward tov, especially in churches.

A DEEP DESIRE FOR TOV

We assume you are reading this because you long to see your church's culture pivot toward tov, and that you became interested in transformation because of some toxic elements at work in your church community.

A *tov* church is one where God's goodness permeates the institution, empowering its members—by God's grace—to become people shaped by God's design, which is Christlikeness (or Christoformity). Tov people, Christlike people, are characterized by empathy, grace, putting other people first, truth telling, justice, and service. Such Christlikeness shows itself in passages like Mark 10:42-45 and Philippians 2:6-11, but also in Jesus' interactions with others, his life, his trial, his death, his resurrection, and his ascension.

> Tov *is the Hebrew word for* good *or* goodness. *God is good, all that God creates is good, all creation has a tov design, and all humans are called by God to do* good. *Jesus embodies goodness, and one aspect of the fruit of the Spirit is goodness. The gospel itself is good (tov) news.*

Is it easy to transform a deeply unhealthy culture into one that reflects God's goodness? Hardly. As one pastor after another has said to me (Scot), "Church culture transformation is not for the faint of heart."

No, it's not easy. But when has radical transformation ever been easy, painless, or quick? We hear the apostle Paul say, "I strike a blow to my body and make it my slave so that after I have preached to others, I myself will not be disqualified for the prize" (1 Corinthians 9:27). He means that the prize is worth the pain, the effort, the time. We also hear Paul say to a beloved church in dire need of culture transformation, "My dear children, for whom I am again in the pains of childbirth until Christ is formed in you . . ." (Galatians 4:19). Paul compares the work of transforming an unhealthy church culture to the terrible pain a woman suffers in childbirth. Easy, painless, and quick? Far from it. So why does he do it? For the beautiful result it produces!

Until Christ is formed in you. That's tov! That is the pivot we desperately need! Transforming a deeply unhealthy culture into a Christlike one, for God's glory and our benefit, is worth every bit of pain, effort, and time it may take.

Are you ready to get to work?

TRANSFORMATION IS POSSIBLE, BUT NOT EASY

IT IS POSSIBLE FOR YOUR church culture to pivot, and to be transformed out of its lingering and seemingly incurable toxicity.

It isn't easy to transform a culture! It's *hard work*. And yet it's well worth the considerable effort required. Consider the story of one church that decided to shift from an attractional culture model to a spiritual formation and transformation model.

THE JOURNEY OF OAK HILLS

Oak Hills Church began simply and modestly in 1984 with seventeen people in a strip mall in suburban Folsom, California. Over the next six years, the church grew to about 200 in weekly attendance, but according to founding pastor Kent Carlson, "There was a sense among the church leadership that something was not quite right."[1] Though most of their growth came from people moving into the area, these were mostly churchgoers looking for a new local church. "We had not seen many new believers become a part of our church," Carlson said.[2]

Around this time, Willow Creek Community Church was emerging as a leader in the church-growth movement with their electric, relevant weekend seeker-services. The leaders of Oak Hills attended a conference at Willow and soon adopted the attractional model as their own.

Attendance exploded, and by 1997 the church grew to an average attendance of 1,700. That's when Kent Carlson hired Mike Lueken as pastor of spiritual formation. By 2002, the two men were senior co-pastors of Oak Hills.

In *Renovation of the Church*, Carlson describes Oak Hills' rapid growth in the 1990s: "It was exhilarating and intoxicating. We would finish a service and there would be a long line of people waiting to talk with me."[3] He also confesses, "The fact that I was recognized [by Willow Creek] as an up-and-coming leader in the seeker-targeted movement filled me with a sense of inflated importance."[4]

But a creeping unease began to grow among the Oak Hills staff. In fact, they collectively used the metaphor of "a monster" to describe their concerns:

> One of the undeniable truths of the culture of the large entrepreneurial, attractional-model church is that it requires constant feeding. When we structure a church around attracting people to cutting-edge, entertaining, interesting, inspirational and always-growing services and ministries, there is simply no room for letting up. . . . There is no resting. If there is a particularly wonderful experience one weekend, we are driven to do even better the next. . . .
>
> Many in our staff . . . were often troubled by the fact that we could never really let up. We would talk about how we could hear the monster beginning to stir again in the fictional basement of our church, and we knew that if we did not feed it, its cage would not hold it. . . . Therefore, week after week, we all mustered the energy to put on the show one more time.[5]

Don't misunderstand: Carlson isn't bashing Willow Creek. The strategy that worked at Willow had also worked at Oak Hills. But although counting attendance numbers and giving are important, they cannot tell the whole story. Nor do they reveal anything about transformed lives or Christlike character.

Eventually, Carlson and Lueken, along with their staff, underwent a process of Spirit-led transformation. The story at Oak Hills began to change, from one that followed a model of success based on numbers and religious consumerism, to one that focused more on God's Kingdom, the mission of the gospel, and spiritual formation in the congregation.

Identifying the Problem

What inspired the profound unease felt by the Oak Hills staff? Individually and as a group, they had discovered the profound, soulful writings of Eugene Peterson, Henri Nouwen, Richard Foster, and Dallas Willard. These deep thinkers "began to infect our minds with so many thought viruses," says Kent Carlson, "that we found ourselves in an almost constant state of ecclesiastical disequilibrium. . . . We began to realize that our current church structure was actually *working against* the invitation of Christ to experience his authentic transformation."[6]

It was this illuminating insight that prompted Oak Hills to begin a process of transformation, which meant building an entirely new foundation based not on how many people were coming but on *who they were becoming.* The leaders bravely confronted perhaps the most difficult challenge of all—their own character, complicity, and duplicity. Mike Lueken writes:

> When we try to attract people by intimating that our church offers something better than the other church, we are complicit in the whole sorry mess of consumer Christianity. We are now stuck in this wearisome game of keeping these people satisfied so they don't go to another church.
>
> KENT CARLSON,
> *RENOVATION OF THE CHURCH*

It was time to face ourselves. It was time to deal with . . . the
ugliness of our motivations, the size of our egos and our
runaway ambition. . . .

We needed to experiment with simplicity. We needed
to deal with our anger and lust. We needed to learn how
to abandon the outcome of our work. . . . We had to
rigorously pursue our own formation. From the beginning,
the transition at Oak Hills had to begin with God doing
something real in our hearts.[7]

Services slowly transformed as well. The pastors began to teach
attenders how to grow in Christ rather than to passively consume an
hour-long show. Lueken explains:

This theme of transformation was woven into nearly all
of our sermons. . . . Regardless of the sermon topic, our
message was essentially the same: cooperate with the Spirit
of God to put off the old, put on the new and become the
person Jesus redeemed you to be. . . .

With glaring redundancy, we concluded our messages by
encouraging people to spend unhurried time in solitude and
silence, cultivating intimacy with Jesus. We were absolutely
convinced spiritual formation in Christ was the key to living
as God intended.[8]

Worship now centered on the story of God rather than putting on
stage what would attract the most people.

Tumult

Doesn't all this sound very tov-ish? But let's not overlook the dif-
ficulty of bringing about this level of change. Oak Hills' let's-do-
all-this-starting-now transition to culture transformation brought
tumultuous times to the church. Several members and some staff
mourned the loss of familiar services and resisted leadership's new
direction. Oak Hills' attendance declined by approximately 1,000

people. Many church employees found the changes difficult because they had been hired to produce and perform. They were utterly confused by the new spiritual formation model. Attenders who had "shopped" for a church and expected to find what they wanted at Oak Hills now didn't know which end was up.

One Step at a Time

In their implementation, the church wisely took small steps. Carlson and Lueken taught spiritual formation from the pulpit and steadily pushed against the spirit of consumerism. Small groups that valued intentionality and developed practices for living like Jesus became an important catalyst for spiritual transformation. Step by step and little by little, the church walked together into a spiritual transformation culture.

> We would never do a very good job of inviting people to reorient their lives around the teachings of Christ if our worship services became simply another place where Christians exercised their consumer choices.
>
> KENT CARLSON,
> RENOVATION OF THE CHURCH

You might wonder what became of Oak Hills' evangelistic passion, modeled after Willow Creek's. It, too, underwent transformation.

As the focus moved from emphasizing numbers, success, and getting new people in the door, Lueken says the church struggled with questions such as "How do we evangelize without being concerned with the numerical growth of the church?" and "How do we invite people into the community of faith without getting caught up in whether or not they are coming to *our* church?"[9] And also this profound question: "How do we evangelize people into a life of apprenticeship to Jesus?"[10]

Evangelism morphed from drawing a crowd to trying to develop the character of Christ within the church. "We discovered," writes Lueken, "that the most important strategy for reaching lost people is Christians living Christianly. Effective evangelism starts by cooperating with God to become a new kind of person out of whom new and better things routinely and easily flow."[11]

A Learning Experience

Carlson and Lueken are honest about the many mistakes they made during the journey of transforming their church's deeply entrenched culture. They confess to moving too quickly and making top-down decisions that ignored questions and lacked compassion. They mention their own impatience and defensiveness, and a tendency to speak instead of listen when parishioners shared their concerns, fears, sorrow, and loss of the familiar.

Carlson and Lueken sought, however imperfectly, to teach ordinary people to be transformed by the love and power of Christ. In the Sermon on the Mount, Carlson says, "there's no talk of an organization. There's no building of empires. Jesus simply invites his followers to live together in the reality of God's kingdom."[12]

> *Effective evangelism starts by cooperating with God to become a new kind of person out of whom new and better things routinely and easily flow.*
>
> MIKE LUEKEN

Though the Oak Hills story is just one example, it illustrates every important practice of church culture transformation that Laura and I have identified as we've studied, read, talked, and listened to pastors over the past three years. And it also shines a bright spotlight on one practice that may do more than anything else to transform a church from unhealthy to tov: spiritual conversation.

THE VITAL IMPORTANCE OF CONVERSATION

Did you notice how conversational the process was at Oak Hills Church? Carlson and Lueken talked to one another, the leaders talked to one another, and members of the congregation talked with one another, with the leaders, and with Carlson and Lueken.

Genuine transformation will require countless conversations, deeply immersed in transparency and honesty. Without open, honest, *safe* conversations—many, many conversations, and not a few of them difficult—there will be no transformation.

Do you know one of the most revealing methods of understanding your coworkers? Invite a conversation by asking good, honest, open questions that people can answer or discuss in safety and mutual respect—with a heart for true exploration. Alas, we are not very good at conversation these days in our society, are we?

Churches are too often known for a different kind of communication style: a tell-others-what-to-do style. This didactic approach springs from a long-standing emphasis in the church on biblical expertise, and the tendency of some to believe it's their job to teach everyone else what to think. But good conversations—involving back-and-forth exchanges through which we learn from one another and gain real understanding—*are required if the church wants to engage in culture transformation.* This may be the most significant need in transformational churches: Members must be able to converse with one another, honestly and with great transparency.

Let this be said: Sometimes (and perhaps more often than not), the best ideas for church culture transformation arise from the congregation. Unfortunately, many pastors, elders, deacons, and other leaders dismiss, disagree with, dispute, and silence those best ideas—which may well be a form of quenching the Spirit. Those who embrace (as we do) "the priesthood of all believers" should be the ones who listen the most to others in the congregation. Careful listening and honest dialogue will lead to new, fruitful, and creative conversations.

SEVEN ATTRIBUTES OF A GOOD CONVERSATION

Good conversations exhibit at least seven attributes. Let's consider each of them in turn.

1. *Good conversations are safe for everyone involved.* Everyone has an opportunity to speak their mind and know that their views are respected.
2. *Good conversations begin with good questions about important topics.* A good conversation is not idle chatter about hither and yon in the by-and-by. It has substance, focus, and direction, and it's about things that matter.

3. *Good conversations are characterized by courtesy and civility.*
   At the least, courtesy and civility mean not interrupting each
   other, not shouting each other down, and not calling each
   other names. Too often we've gotten away from common
   courtesy in the church, and social media makes it even
   worse. In good conversations about the church, Christians
   can learn a new way of civility.

4. *Good conversations occur in a spirit of exploration and
   experimentation.* We identify a topic—transforming
   church culture—that more and more people recognize
   is of colossal importance, and we start asking questions:
   What *is* the current culture? What are its strengths
   and weaknesses? What problems does it present? How
   can we move the culture toward tov? As people answer
   these questions, probe one another's answers, and
   explore together what goodness may mean for the church,
   progress is made toward a positive transformation of
   culture.

5. *Good conversations are on a mutual quest for wisdom.* Good
   conversations often tend to be about something that is not
   yet known or that needs to be learned. Where a know-it-
   all may try to direct and coerce a conversation toward a
   predetermined conclusion, good conversationalists allow
   the give-and-take to germinate ideas and lead toward
   conclusions moderated by careful thinking.

6. *Good conversations discipline themselves to stay on topic.*
   They avoid wandering off to Twitter's latest scandal or the
   church griper's latest complaint. If the topic is tov, they
   stick to tov.

7. *Good conversations in the church require shared convictions
   about Christian truth (gospel), relationships (love), and goals
   (wisdom).* The time may well come for white-hot debates.
   Church culture transformation will, at times, set people off.
   Our concern here is not that every conversation be calm
   and reasonable, but that the heart of the conversation be

finding common ground. Learning to think about culture and transformation by looking at a variety of scenarios can nudge us toward tov. Genuine conversations may well reveal that what many considered a shared conviction is not, in fact, shared by all.[13]

Warm Up

Consider two fictional scenarios for a conversation:

1. You are a fairly new staff member at your church. You know people's names and they know yours. One day you notice the pastor step into a nearby office and you hear raised voices. You wonder what's going on. Soon the pastor shuts the door—rather, he slams it—and storms off. You think, *Someone's having a bad day.* A month later you witness something similar. You decide to talk about it with a trusted friend on staff, and she tells you she's seen the same behavior off and on for the last five years. You wonder how a pastor can act like that. In a moment of consternation, you realize that others must have witnessed such things before, and you wonder how people in the church permit such behavior. *Why doesn't anyone seem to have the courage to confront the pastor?*

   a. How would you describe the culture at work in this scenario?
   b. What single biggest problem does it suggest to you? Why?
   c. How open would you be to someone confronting *you*?
   d. What would you do to form a more tov culture?

2. Anne is a teacher at a private Christian school. She has taught there since its founding, working for several principals during her tenure. In recent years, Anne has noticed changes in the school but doesn't quite have the language to describe them. The latest new principal who was hired seems friendly, warm, and helpful in public. But Anne has begun to hear stories about colleagues getting their hands slapped by the principal for minor offenses, and it has become increasingly common to find teachers in tears in their classrooms after school. Also, some staff members who were called in by administration and released from their positions had to sign nondisclosure documents prohibiting them from explaining why they suddenly left the school. Anne is afraid to be seen speaking to anyone but "approved" and "safe" colleagues. She finds hidden ways to communicate with her teammates so that

she cannot be blamed by leadership for supposedly "being negative." She loves her students but feels overwhelmed with fear—of saying the wrong thing, making a mistake, or upsetting the principal and getting her hand slapped too.

a. How would you describe the culture at work in this scenario?
b. What single biggest problem does it suggest to you? Why?
c. What might be keeping Anne from speaking up?
d. What would you do to form a more tov culture?

Get Some Insight

1. After making sure you can discuss the issue in safety and mutual exploration, have a conversation with a coworker or associate about an area of concern in your organization. Take care that your conversation exhibits all seven of the attributes of a healthy conversation listed on pages 13–15. What did you learn from the conversation? How did the conversation make you feel? Why?

2. What "shared convictions" in your church or organization may not, in fact, be *shared* at all? Give some examples and explain why you think these may not be commonly held convictions.

Do the Hard Work

One of the best ways to begin discerning the culture in your organization or church is to ask some key questions. The answers, at times, may be surprising or even frightening. Pastors, leaders, and staff members will likely be the ones to select the specific questions for discussion, but all stakeholders must make sure the questions are *relevant*.

- Who has power?
- Who answers to whom and why?
- Who gets paid the most?
- What are the gradations of salaries and wages?
- Who gets benefits and perks, what are they, and why do certain people get them?

- Which groups/pockets have the most influence?
- What do various power pockets think of one another?
- What expectations do people have?
- How would you describe the character of your church or institution?
- What are your institution's theological claims and cultural assumptions?

Questions that pertain to others in the organization are often the easiest to answer. We can always see how someone else contributes to or is part of the problem. But it's much harder to answer those same questions about ourselves! We're all practiced at the art of self-deception (see James 1:22-24).

At Oak Hills, Kent Carlson and Mike Lueken asked questions like these:

- What is the purpose of the church?
- How does the church relate to a consumer-driven culture?
- To what extent have we oriented our church around the desires of people who have little interest in living as disciples of Jesus?
- Do our ministry practices proclaim the gospel and further the cause of God's Kingdom?

Conversations based on questions like these will make it possible for you to comprehensively grasp your church's culture, instead of focusing only on what people *see* and *say*—that is, the values and creeds you confess. Honest dialogue will help you to uncover the underlying culture that directly affects the health of your church or organization.

Please remember: This exercise is not a simple "checklist" activity that will take only a few moments to complete before you check it off your list. A proper—and therefore helpful—analysis of your culture will take time and countless conversations, and will often come with a degree of pain. But unless you do the hard work, you will never identify the true culture of your church or organization.

You cannot transform a culture without first completing a comprehensive analysis of where you are now.

CHANGE STARTS WITH THE SOIL

CULTURE HAS ENORMOUS POWER. Transformation is extremely difficult. Candid conversations are essential to the process of becoming tov. Until now we've been talking about *concepts*; maybe we can better describe the nature of the task ahead by using an illustration.

Think of your church or organizational culture as a peach tree with three subcultures:

1. Leaves and fruit
2. Trunk and branches
3. Soil, where the roots do their work

Though each subculture plays a significant role in the production of peaches, the soil determines the health of the entire tree. As with any cultivation process, everything starts with the soil.

Laura and I are not arborists, but we have learned that what happens beneath the surface of the soil is perhaps more important than what happens above. As consumers, we may only care about the

peach itself. (Is it sweet and juicy? Will it satisfy our desires?) But if the soil is contaminated and full of toxins, eventually it will destroy both the tree *and* its fruit.

The visible elements of the peach tree—leaves, flowers, and fruit—correspond to what people can see and experience in your church, ministry, or organization. They come to hear a good preacher and good music professionally produced; see good-looking people on the stage; meet friendly faces at the doors; find lots of ministries for kids, teens, young adults, singles, and families; find adequate parking; and (above all) tap in to an easily available, user-friendly website with online streaming.

In a consumer-driven church culture, that may be all they really care about. They don't want to know what's going on beneath the surface.

But just as every tree's growth—and health—depends significantly on the condition of the soil, so too the growth and health of the church depends on the condition of its "soil"—that is, on the culture in which it exists.

DIGGING INTO THE SOIL

Let's get down on our knees for a bit and dig into that soil. What will we find there? The soil for any church can be tainted by the flesh or led by the Spirit. Sometimes the flesh takes control and makes the soil toxic. Paul's well-known passage on "the acts of the flesh" and "the fruit of the Spirit" is worth meditation:

> The acts of the flesh are obvious: sexual immorality, impurity and debauchery; idolatry and witchcraft; hatred, discord, jealousy, fits of rage, selfish ambition, dissensions, factions and envy; drunkenness, orgies, and the like. I warn you, as I did before, that those who live like this will not inherit the kingdom of God.
>
> But the fruit of the Spirit is love, joy, peace, forbearance, kindness, goodness, faithfulness, gentleness and self-control. Against such things there is no law.
>
> GALATIANS 5:19-23

In our studies of church cultures, the following habits seem to be the predominant indicators of toxicity. These toxic elements tend to grow from a soil steeped in human pride, power, and authority:

- ambition
- competition
- abusive power
- success measured by numbers
- greed
- glory and fame
- consumerism

In recent years, far too much has been revealed about so-called celebrity pastors. But these fleshly habits exist not only in big churches with famous pastors, but also in small churches with relatively unknown leaders. In every case we have seen, the underlying culture—that is, the soil—was toxic. That soil often corrupted its leaders, and then those leaders corrupted untold things within their reach. Does the soil corrupt the leader, or does the leader corrupt the soil? The only accurate answer is *yes*. Both. Most of the time. In specific cases, it may have been the toxic soil; in others, it's the toxic leader.

A common word used to describe corrupted leaders is *narcissistic*. Narcissists typically exhibit a sense of grandiosity, coupled with self-centeredness, insecurity, and lack of empathy. To picture what this might look like, consider another illustration of the peach tree.

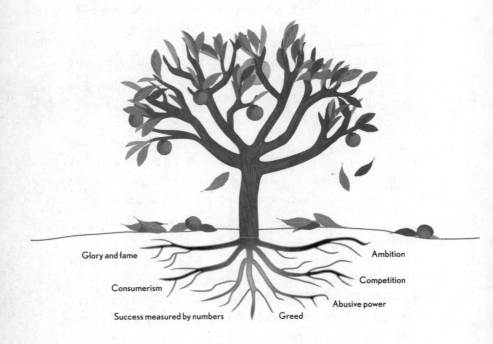

Chuck DeGroat, author of an important book titled *When Narcissism Comes to Church*, provides a brief overview of the kind of narcissistic pastor in whom we would say the above characteristics are alive and *un*well. The problem here is the soil in which a narcissistic pastor grows; that is, the toxic culture around him (or her):

So, how can we tell? We can often tell by monitoring the relational and vocational orbit of a leader. For years, I've observed pastors in a variety of settings. And while some confident and charming pastors may exhibit slight tendencies of narcissism, a larger cluster of features is often seen in diagnosably narcissistic leaders. Expanding on Craig and Carolyn Williford's helpful work on troubled church ministries . . . I suggest these ten features of narcissistic pastors:

- All decision-making centers on them
- Impatience or a lack of ability to listen to others
- Delegating without giving proper authority or with too many limits
- Feelings of entitlement
- Feeling threatened or intimidated by other talented staff
- Needing to be the best and brightest in the room
- Inconsistency and impulsiveness
- Praising and withdrawing
- Intimidation of others
- Fauxnerability (a faux or fake vulnerability)[1]

A healthy church soil makes it difficult for narcissism to poison the ground. But narcissism isn't the only poison found in toxic soil. Psychologist and cultural workplace researcher Paul White has identified three key components of a toxic workplace:

1. Dysfunctional Employees—withholding or distorting information, communicating indirectly, creating conflict and tension, having a sense of entitlement
2. Poor Policies and Procedures—poor communication, unwritten or outdated policies, management circumvention of policies
3. Toxic Leaders—impure motives, narcissistic, manipulative, condescending, inauthentic, extreme focus on goals and appearances, steal credit from others (blame, make excuses, dishonest, create conflict among others).[2]

God wants the Holy Spirit to take control of a church's or Christian organization's culture. One way to look at this is through the fruit of the Spirit described in Galatians 5:22-23. In our studies about the church, we found that those in whom the Holy Spirit was producing the fruit of the Spirit had their hearts shaped by five common character traits:

- A gospel centered on Jesus
- Commitment to the orthodox teachings of the faith
- A life of Spirit-shaped spiritual transformation
- Time-proven faithfulness
- The instinct of love

What's in the soil determines the health of the fruit. Soil contaminated by the flesh produces fleshly fruit (inedible and poisonous). Soil renewed and regenerated by the Spirit produces Spirit-prompted practices and Spirit-infused people.

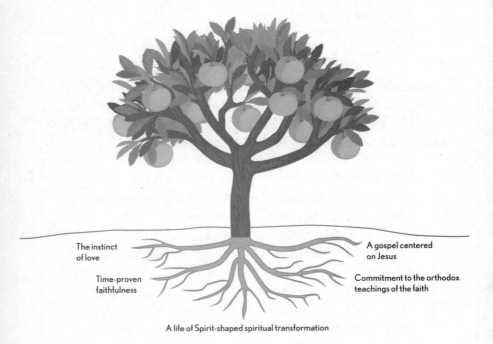

The instinct of love

A gospel centered on Jesus

Time-proven faithfulness

Commitment to the orthodox teachings of the faith

A life of Spirit-shaped spiritual transformation

Every orchard needs an arborist, or an arborist who hires a specialist to discover the health of the soil. Likewise, every church needs informed people—clergy *and* laity—armed with effective tools designed to ascertain the health of the church's soil.

UNFLINCHING ASSESSMENTS

The process of culture transformation cannot begin without an unflinching assessment of your institution's culture. Such an assessment requires a willingness to ask, "What's really in the soil?" We have developed a Tov Tool (see the appendix, page 207) to help your church discover more about its culture.

There are no quick fixes or easy solutions that will immediately reveal the toxins present. We've all learned to live within our church's culture. Culture describes what's normal. Those who are immersed in it often don't recognize what's really there.

You are reading this book for a reason. Maybe you know something's wrong, or maybe you're not sure. But you're probably at least wondering whether something might be askew, something toxic in the character of your congregation or its leaders.

Transforming a culture requires arduous, often painful discovery. It takes a willingness to learn why the tree isn't producing blossoms or why the fruit is rotten or why the blossoms are an unexpected color. It takes sound character, keen curiosity, and resolute courage for the arborist (and tree owner) to accept a candid evaluation.

COURAGE REQUIRED

Courage may be the most important character trait necessary for the practice of discerning your church's culture. Author and political scientist Anne-Marie Slaughter quotes her mentor, David Bradley, about showing courage by facing honestly the criticism coming your way when problems have been exposed.

> "Run toward the criticism." Even if you are 98 percent
> right and only 2 percent wrong, . . . acknowledge the fault
> rather than insist on the virtue. Then use it as the point of
> departure for a "learning journey."[3]

Slaughter describes the process that led her to understand that her organization needed transformation. Facing the criticism head-on led her to personal discoveries about her own character, about how her character influenced her management, and about how her character shaped her use of power. Slaughter writes:

> A crisis . . . pushed me into a process of personal renewal, a
> path that has been exhilarating, rewarding, and hard. It has
> meant running toward the criticism not only in the moment
> but also in terms of looking backward over parts of my life
> and finding negative patterns. It has required building a
> new kind of resilience by reaching out to others and finding
> larger purpose in our daily work, resilience that has helped
> me use some of the criticism I heard as an opportunity for
> change. . . . It has changed the way I lead, or at least try to
> lead: as horizontally as possible, from the center *and* the
> margin. It has changed my understanding of how best to
> exercise power.[4]

It's not easy to accept the truth about our own toxicity, or that of the church we are a part of. We tend to distort what we don't like so that it looks more like what we do like. The existing culture—please hear this—*resists learning the truth about itself.* Quoting again from Edgar Schein:

> The reexamination of basic assumptions temporarily
> destabilizes our cognitive and interpersonal world, releasing
> large quantities of basic anxiety.
>   Rather than tolerating such anxiety levels, we tend to
> want to perceive the events around us as congruent with

our assumptions, even if that means distorting, denying, projecting, or in other ways falsifying to ourselves what may be going on around us. It is in this psychological process that culture has its ultimate power.[5]

In family systems theory, the culture we find comfortable and normal is called *homeostasis*. It encapsulates the sense of normality we feel about how things work in our familiar environments. One can expect resistance to culture transformation because deep-rooted change disrupts homeostasis and creates disequilibrium, leading to disorientation. No matter how toxic the culture may be, people will yearn to return to homeostasis.

LISTEN WELL

If you ask the kinds of questions mentioned in the "Getting to Work" section at the end of this chapter, you will hear some good and some not-so-good responses. To pivot and transform a culture, you have to know where you're starting from, because transformation can only happen if it is congruent with the existing culture.

To understand your church's DNA you will need to ask questions, listen to the answers, ponder what you've been told, compare results with others, and discuss your findings with key transformation agents. Listening will likely mean facing some tough realities.

What happens if, through listening and learning, you find high levels of dysfunction, lack of trust, or power abuses in your church? Are you willing to own what needs to be owned and change what needs to be changed?

VULNERABILITY REQUIRED

Christian workplaces often reveal their true culture—that is, not in the way they expect—when they provide cultural surveys to their staff. A woman staff member recently told me of some serious tension at her church over its treatment of women. The director above her decided to do a survey, which gave the women a sense of relief and hope. The survey went out . . . and they heard nothing . . . for almost a year.

When they finally received some feedback, it was a good—but begrudging and minimal—response, indicating that the leaders had heard the women but were not about to acknowledge that the suggested changes were in response to the women's concerns. In short, another indicator of the underlying problem!

We also have seen leaders in Christian workplaces ask everyone to fill out a survey but then hide the results, blame the staff for poor ratings, or manipulate people into rating the organization at the highest levels. We have been told of workplaces hiding poor survey results from the larger community, denying the existence of negative feedback, and even gaslighting whistleblowers who ask to see the results. When an employee takes a culture survey and trusts the employer to do something with the results, but then sees the employer behave dishonorably with those results, it should surprise no one that morale deteriorates and trust dissolves.

It takes emotional and cultural health to hear the truth, accept it as reality, and make the necessary adjustments to bring about positive change.

We don't mean to suggest that culture surveys are the be-all and end-all answer to assessing your church's health, nor are we recommending only one specific survey. But it's important to understand that *transforming a culture requires an honest and comprehensive understanding of the organization's cultural DNA*. And that requires some expertise and probably some means of information gathering.

The larger point here is the importance of an unwavering commitment to transparency and truth, to learning and listening, to confession and accountability, to humility and a willingness to be transformed, and to allowing reality to shape and inform your next steps.

RADICALLY DIFFERENT AND QUITE HEALTHY

Only a foolish arborist would soak the soil with inorganic chemicals and imagine that good will come of it. A toxic chemical can destroy

both the ecosystem *and* the tree. And once the soil has been corrupted, it can take a *long* time to restore it to health.

Can it be done? Yes. Will it be difficult? Yes. Will it be pleasant?
Not usually. But is it worth all the effort? To answer that question, let
me quote a pastor, John Rosensteel, who faced just such a daunting
task when he was called to a new church in a new city:

> I had spent eighteen years at a church that was very healthy.
> We vetted the [new] church well and knew it was a fixer-
> upper (we had no idea). One thing I have learned is that
> things are usually far worse than they appear. The last six
> years have been the most demanding years I have ever spent
> in ministry. We came to realize the church was so unhealthy,
> and evil in places, that we would need to take it all the way
> down to the studs and do a complete rebirth. There are very
> few resources in the church world that provide wisdom on
> rebirths or re-culturing. For this reason, we had to seek
> out people who had done it and learn from the business
> and sports world, which was helpful, but the wisdom didn't
> always apply. But by God's grace, six years in, our church is
> radically different and quite healthy.[6]

Yes, it's worth it. And by God's grace, it's more than possible for
you as well.

Warm Up

1. What are the "leaves" and "fruit" in your church or organization?

2. What is the "trunk" of your church or organization?

3. Describe the "soil" of your church or organization, where the roots do their work.

4. Read Galatians 5:19-21. What elements listed here do you see in your church or organization? How may you be contributing to any of these?

5. Read Galatians 5:22-23. What elements listed here do you see in your church or organization? How may you be contributing to any of these?

Get Some Insight

1. Which of the "toxic soil" habits listed on page 21 do you see in your organization? Explain.

2. Which of Chuck DeGroat's "ten features of narcissistic" leaders listed on page 23 do you see in your organization? List any relevant features and explain why you listed them.

3. Ask a friend, coworker, or someone who reports to you to identify which, if any, of the ten characteristics of narcissism on page 23 you tend to exhibit.

4. Which of Paul White's three components of a toxic workplace listed on page 23 do you see in your organization? List any relevant components and explain why you listed them.

5. Which of the heart-shaping character traits listed on page 24 appear evident in your organization? Which ones are absent or minimal? How are you contributing to the problems or the solutions?

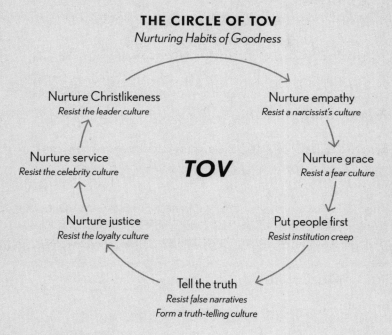

THE CIRCLE OF TOV
Nurturing Habits of Goodness

Nurture Christlikeness
Resist the leader culture

Nurture empathy
Resist a narcissist's culture

Nurture service
Resist the celebrity culture

TOV

Nurture grace
Resist a fear culture

Nurture justice
Resist the loyalty culture

Put people first
Resist institution creep

Tell the truth
Resist false narratives
Form a truth-telling culture

Do the Hard Work

Ask the following difficult questions, first about yourself and then about your church or organization, and listen thoughtfully to the responses you receive. Have some honest back-and-forth conversations. The goal is not to be *right*, but to discover what's really going on in the soil of your church or organization. Any of the following questions, based on our Circle of Tov, can help you to discover what toxins may lurk in that soil.

- Which of our policies, programs, and structures are producing tov? Which are creating toxicity?
- Am I perceived as empathetic?
- Are we perceived as an empathetic organization?

- Am I perceived as grace-giving and grace-receiving?
- Are we perceived as a grace-giving and grace-receiving organization?
- Am I perceived as a "people first" person?
- Are we perceived as a "people first" organization?
- Am I perceived as a truth teller?
- Are we perceived as a truth-telling organization?
- Am I perceived as someone who does what is right at the right time?
- Are we perceived as a community that does what is right at the right time?
- Am I perceived as a servant?
- Are we a servant-shaped organization?
- Am I growing in Christlikeness?
- Are we a Christlike organization?

These questions, along with many others you could ask, will make it possible for you to comprehensively grasp your church's culture, instead of only looking at what people see (the fruit, the leaves, the branches, and the trunk). They will help you uncover the underlying "cultural soil" that so greatly affects the health of your peach tree.

PART 1

THREE
PIVOTAL
PRIORITIES

3

FORM TOV CHARACTER

VIRTUE, OR CHARACTER, has more lasting influence than giftedness or skill. As Noah Webster, one of America's founders, said, "The *virtues* of men are of more consequence to society than their *abilities*, and for this reason the *heart* should be cultivated with more [diligence] than the *head*."[1]

Issues of power will always be at the center of a pivot away from toxic to tov. That's why it's important to understand that *character* is what matters most in the use of power, in the transformation of a culture, and in all the practices we discuss in this book. Power tied to lack of character leads to spiritual abuse. Power wedded to godly character produces a Christlike church culture. We will discuss this in greater detail in chapter 4.

FROM SKILL TO CHARACTER

Character formation, if implemented in the church, would create a revolution more than a reformation. *Revolution* is the right word because it would turn the current reality on its head. For too long, churches have measured and valued and glorified *who gets stuff done*, rather than who exhibits godly character. Especially in the past fifty years, too many churches have hired on the basis of talents and skills and the capacity to "bring it" for weekend services. Churches by and large do *not* hire on the basis of character.

Somehow, we have equated *ability* with *character*. But when ability replaces character, we get toxicity in the boardroom and in the pulpit, and those toxicities corrupt the entire culture, whether corporate or church. If you examine the job descriptions used in searches for pastors, associate pastors, and church staff (as we have), you will find (as we did) an absence of expressed interest in character and a profusion of terms connected to skills. Job descriptions, even for senior pastors, have devolved into can-do lists.

I (Scot) am a bird-watcher. Watching birds can teach us many lessons, one of which is that aggressiveness and size matter. A 2021 *Washington Post* article described a hierarchy of aggression among birds. And the winner is . . . the American crow! But the crow finds company among other aggressive birds such as common grackles, red-bellied woodpeckers, and blue jays. Which birds stand by and wait their turn? Chickadees, goldfinches, and dark-eyed juncos.[2]

You know where I'm going with this, don't you? Churches have a nasty habit of hiring crows while ignoring the goldfinches. In other words, an aggressive personality trumps tov character.

In *The Ascent of a Leader*, which explores the topic of character in leadership, Bill Thrall, Bruce McNicol, and Ken McElrath compare a "capacity ladder" with a "character ladder." The former is a "task-driven organization, at the expense of people" and creates "people-users," while a character ladder focuses on people and their success. On the capacity ladder, accountability means getting things done. Character, by contrast, focuses on depth of influence, living the truth, and protecting relationships. It sees failures in terms of development, not immediate results.

The authors describe a character-shaped leader and a culture of relationships and grace in ascending terms: (1) trusting God and others, leading to humility; (2) choosing vulnerability, leading to submission; (3) aligning with truth, leading to obedience; (4) paying the price, leading to suffering and maturity; which then results in the ability to (5) discover your destiny.[3]

The ancient Greeks put the modern church to shame, for their philosophers taught and strove for character development, something we call "virtue ethics" today. For Aristotle, "we become just by doing just acts, temperate by doing temperate acts, brave by doing brave acts."[4] Building on Aristotle's thought, public policy expert James Q. Wilson writes, "Moral virtue is the same as good character, and a good character is formed not through moral instruction or personal self-discovery but through the regular repetition of right actions."[5] The big idea is that if we practice something often enough, it becomes an instinct produced in our character. When transferred to ethics and morality, if we do good, if we act with courage, if we are self-disciplined in our desires long enough, then goodness, courage, and discipline will become habits. A person's deepest habits form his or her character. Aristotle developed these concepts; his teachings passed into the Roman world and then into the church.

By the time Richard Foster wrote *Celebration of Discipline* in 1978, the term *disciplines* had become a Christian word for virtue ethics. Dallas Willard picked up this theme in his books, including *The Spirit of the Disciplines* (1988), which explores the concept of character transformation. These authors, and others, pleaded with the church to shift away from valuing talent, skill, and glitz to do the deep work of forming Christlike character.[6]

But let's face it: These authors did not win the day, and character formation has yet to become the heart of what most churches do. What Foster, Willard, and others explained so clearly has not become central to ministry job descriptions. The result? We find ourselves right back where we were. We value the highly skilled, the most talented, the most magnetic . . . and what do we get? Talented, magnetic people. As for character, it may come with the package, but it's not necessarily required or found. We don't value good character highly enough. Because we're more interested in great platform speakers, talented musicians, and attractive leaders, we wind up with skillful people who leave behind a wake of broken relationships. They lack significant character, because character often "doesn't platform well."

Maybe the platform is the problem?

Churches that want to transform their culture away from platforming to character formation must reshape their priorities toward tov. They must begin to work from new foundations.

Culture transformation *is* possible, but not without transformation of character.

DEFINING CHARACTER

Let's start with a brief definition: "Character denotes the particular set of qualities, both natural and acquired, that serves to identify a person or community. These qualities . . . will be manifest as a consistency of action that can be termed 'integrity.'"[7] The authors of this definition, Michael Cox and Brad Kallenberg, continue in the same vein: "Accordingly, in the context of Christian ethics, character names an established disposition (or set of dispositions) with respect to the particular conception of the human good exemplified by Christ. Such character is developed over time and, as such, can be formed either toward or away from virtues, understood as those intellectual and affective habits that enable the pursuit of excellence"[8] Our shorthand way of expressing the "good exemplified by Christ" is tov.

Christian integrity measures how consistently a person's words and actions align with his or her character, as compared to the life of Jesus. Christian character, therefore, looks like this: *One's basic personality, shaped or unshaped over time by virtue or vice, resulting in consistent moral traits exhibited by that person.*

We should be asking whether our churches prioritize character formation or place a higher value on performance. Though in practice the answer fluctuates between the two ends of the spectrum, from our many conversations with pastors and congregants over the past three years, we are convinced that retooling most churches to prioritize character formation takes more than a mere shift or change. It requires transformation—a revolution rather than a reformation.

THE BIBLE AND CHARACTER

Jesus taught that a good tree (good character) produces good fruit. Bad character eventually reveals itself as rotten fruit, while good character over time will manifest itself as a sweet, juicy peach. Hear the words of Jesus:

> By their fruit you will recognize them. Do people pick grapes from thornbushes, or figs from thistles? Likewise, every good tree bears good fruit, but a bad tree bears bad fruit. A good tree cannot bear bad fruit, and a bad tree cannot bear good fruit. Every tree that does not bear good fruit is cut down and thrown into the fire. Thus, by their fruit you will recognize them.
> MATTHEW 7:16-20

Though this isn't hard to understand, some go too far with it. No human *always* produces juicy peaches, any more than someone *always* produces rotten fruit. Even as Christians, we don't always behave in good ways. Therefore, Jesus, who was always tov, exhorts his followers to examine themselves and others. That is, he wants us to become "fruit inspectors."

Jesus also talked about character formation using the term *heart*. Again, consider his words:

> The words you speak come from the heart—that's what defiles you. For from the heart come evil thoughts, murder, adultery, all sexual immorality, theft, lying, and slander.
> MATTHEW 15:18-19, NLT

Though Jesus didn't use the word *ethos* (character), so central to the philosophy of Aristotle, what he teaches is similar: Our behavior expresses our character. That is, within reasonable limits, what we do tells others who we are.

In the writings of the apostle Paul, the indwelling of the Holy Spirit becomes the central reality of transformation. For instance, consider

Romans 5:5: "Hope does not put us to shame, because God's love has been poured out into our hearts through the Holy Spirit, who has been given to us." Further, in Romans 8:9, Paul says, "You . . . are not in the realm of the flesh but are in the realm of the Spirit, if indeed the Spirit of God lives in you. And if anyone does not have the Spirit of Christ, they do not belong to Christ." And in 1 Corinthians 3:16, Paul indicates that this Spirit-in-us is working not only individually or personally, but in the church corporately: "Don't you know that you yourselves are God's temple and that God's Spirit dwells in your midst?"

Jesus and the apostles all believed in the inner work of transformation, or character formation, which produces good fruit, or what we often today call *virtue*. Paul captures the essence of this virtue in 2 Corinthians 3:17-18:

> Now the Lord is the Spirit, and where the Spirit of the Lord is, there is freedom. And we all, who with unveiled faces contemplate the Lord's glory, are being transformed into his image with ever-increasing glory, which comes from the Lord, who is the Spirit.

The ultimate virtue is *Christlikeness*. The Spirit *in* us transforms us into the image of Christ.

Cox and Kallenberg offer a practical observation of how this transformation takes place. We urge you to read this slowly:

> Discipleship entails the transformation of the self, effected through the repetition of particular practices—for example, the Eucharist, prayer, evangelism, hospitality, care for the poor, confession, forgiveness, worship—which, when properly undertaken, help to fashion the Christian's character in the likeness of Jesus.[9]

Though we like this statement very much, we want to draw out the phrase "when properly undertaken" (and thus anticipate the "energy source" of transformation we will discuss in part 3).

Even excellent habits and practices won't transform us into looking like Jesus if we don't tap into God's grace and the power of the
Spirit. Neither can we ignore the powerful influence of models in
our congregations or relationships. Good practices and wonderful
models are not enough; we need the grace of God in the power of
the Spirit.

Character matters more than culture. Character matters more
than strategy. It is character that determines the very substance of
where we're headed. As one pastor friend said to us recently, "The
question is, 'Who are we becoming?'"

If character matters this much, then we must ask: Where do we
begin? How do we kick-start a transformation of church culture with
a deeper concentration on character? It takes a lifetime (and beyond)
to fully form Christlikeness in us, but we can see progress by looking
at four categories of transformation: (1) know yourself; (2) learn the
virtues; (3) develop personal character; and (4) cultivate character
within a congregation.

KNOW YOURSELF

We agree with the many psychologists, some of whom teach in seminaries, who say that every person must become self-aware. If we
could have our wish, churches would not hire any pastor or staff
person without the candidate first taking a personality evaluation
and discussing the results with a trained person who would advise
the search committee.

Many tests, inventories, and
evaluations are available, from
the intense MMPI (Minnesota
Multiphasic Personality Inventory)
administered by a trained psychologist to the Myers-Briggs Type

> *The least emphasized but most
> important strength needed for
> a minister is self-awareness.*
> EMILY HUNTER McGOWIN

Indicator and the Enneagram. The more pop approaches can easily
be misused, but when evaluated by discerning mentors, any of these
systems can help people become more self-aware.

Another way of evaluating self-awareness has to do with learning our strengths and weaknesses. Again, various instruments can help here. One that we value is the VIA Character Strengths Survey (https://www.viacharacter.org/)—a quick, online form that can be completed at no cost.[10] We urge you to use the VIA, or another such survey, and discuss it with your closest colleagues. If you all do it together, it will feel safer for everyone.

We can *all* broaden our self-awareness by locating ourselves on a scale of our cultural awareness. The ones most responsible for culture formation and for culture transformation are those most in need of self-awareness.

LEARN THE VIRTUES OF THE FAITH

If the first step in character formation is self-awareness, the second step is to study what the Bible teaches about character and virtue— and then to practice these things.

Christopher Peterson and Martin Seligman, in a well-regarded study of character strengths, identified six basic categories of human virtues that transcend time and culture:

- wisdom and knowledge
- courage
- humanity
- justice
- temperance
- transcendence (which is not so much about God as getting outside of ourselves)[11]

These virtues find their origins in Plato and Aristotle, but they can help us think about distinctly *Christian* virtues—which both overlap the list above and shift our focus to different domains. We long for church cultures to transform toward tov, and for that, we must practice these specifically Christian virtues.

Some tend to lock down on a single image of the moral life found in the Bible and make everything fit that image. We believe the Bible offers at least five major avenues for teaching the virtuous (or good) life. That is, the Bible provides *on-ramps* for teaching character. Each can be used to great profit in discipleship, but we need them all, not just one. The Big Five are readily identifiable:

1. The Ten Commandments (Exodus 20:1-17; Deuteronomy 5:6-21)
2. The ethical categories of the prophets, epitomized by Micah 6:8:

> He has told you, O mortal, what is good;
>   and what does the LORD require of you
> but *to do justice and to love kindness,*
>   *and to walk humbly with your God?*[12]

3. Jesus' Sermon on the Mount/Plain (Matthew 5:1–7:29; Luke 6:20-49)
4. Life in the Spirit (Romans 5–8; Galatians 5:16-26)
5. Master categories: love, godliness, justice, tov

Note especially that Christian virtues are learned and practiced *in community.*[13] These are not solo ethics; they are developed and practiced in the life of the church.

Let us not overlook the immense value of Paul's exposition of life in the Spirit in Galatians 5:16-26. Think of it in terms of forming character, both individually and as a congregation.

> So I say, walk by the Spirit, and you will not gratify the desires of the flesh. For the flesh desires what is contrary to the Spirit, and the Spirit what is contrary to the flesh. They are in conflict with each other, so that you are not to do whatever you want. But if you are led by the Spirit, you are not under the law.

The acts of the flesh are obvious: sexual immorality, impurity and debauchery; idolatry and witchcraft; hatred, discord, jealousy, fits of rage, selfish ambition, dissensions, factions and envy; drunkenness, orgies, and the like. I warn you, as I did before, that those who live like this will not inherit the kingdom of God.

But the fruit of the Spirit is love, joy, peace, forbearance, kindness, goodness, faithfulness, gentleness and self-control. Against such things there is no law. Those who belong to Christ Jesus have crucified the flesh with its passions and desires. Since we live by the Spirit, let us keep in step with the Spirit. Let us not become conceited, provoking and envying each other.

What can we add that hasn't been said before? Nothing. But consider a few points worth remembering.

1. *The empowering presence of the Spirit matters more than the specific fruit.* Just as a peach grows through a combination of nutrients in the soil, the sun, and oxygen, we grow through the inner working of the Holy Spirit in our lives. We call these virtues "the fruit *of the Spirit*" because it is the Spirit who produces them.

2. *Each segment of the fruit of the Spirit is relational and requires others.* There is no obsession here with individual solitude and personal intimacy with God. Instead, this is all about the Spirit at work in *us* so we can learn to live with *one another*. In that way, we become a culture of the Spirit's fruit, together acting as agents of God's Spirit.

3. *Love is the cornerstone.* Why love? Why not joy, peace, or kindness? Because love ties all the fruit into a bundle of Christlike character.

4. *The fruit of the Spirit stands in stark contrast to the alternative, "the acts of the flesh."* For Paul, the Spirit is in a daily, till-the-end-of-your-life battle with the flesh. On earth, sometimes the flesh prevails.

5. *We are to do some things because we can*. Notice the verbs Paul uses to show us what God requires of us:

- *walk* by the Spirit (verse 16)
- *be led* by the Spirit (verse 18)
- *live* by the Spirit (verse 25)
- *keep in step* with the Spirit (verse 25)

Transformation occurs through the Spirit as he works in us—in our walking, being led, living, and stepping—and as he transforms us into agents of the Spirit's fruit. Unless we *practice* tov, the Spirit-empowered character of Christlikeness will not be formed in us.

What a sad commentary on the Christian church that we have memorized and mastered a lone Bible verse about goodness: "There is no one righteous, not even one."[14] By emphasizing this dire description, we ignore that God created us as good; we made things bad; and then God redeemed us to do and become good. Focusing on our fallenness tramples on the truth that Jesus is the Good Shepherd who calls us to good works, and that goodness is a fruit of the Spirit. We have somehow obscured all this goodness by focusing on one depressing description.

Does it strike you that the late bishop Desmond Tutu would be so bold as to title his book *Made for Goodness*?[15] We stand with Tutu: We *were* made for goodness and we *are still* made for goodness. Tov is the direction of God's transforming energies in us.

DEVELOP PERSONAL CHARACTER

Though church culture transformation requires a revolution at the level of community, it begins at a personal, individual level. Each person involved in corporate transformation must keep in mind the following principles:

1. *If character formation lies at the heart of church culture transformation, we must pivot to programs that develop character.* Too many such programs concentrate on practicing disciplines without giving sufficient attention to character.

2. *Programs that are community-oriented (that is, not too individualistic) will benefit and encourage the spiritual formation of the congregation.* Tov character describes how people relate to God and to one another. A truly tov character, then, loves God and loves others. Some Christian thinkers have broken through the individualism plaguing virtue ethics and have shaped character in the context of community.[16] The transformation of an individual into Christlikeness, into tov, is a transformation into the virtues that help the community flourish.

3. *Tov-formed mentors must work with those who need more tov formation.* Corrupted characters energized by toxic carnality will stunt the formation of goodness in those they mentor. Tov as a character trait is caught and absorbed more than taught or programmed.

4. *Mentors must avoid coercive conversations, demands on the mentees, and any kind of seemingly secretive "discernment revelation."* While trust between mentor and mentee is required, trust takes time; and trust can be destroyed if the mentors are not themselves growing in tov. You can't rush character formation, which means that the trust between mentor and mentee must be well deserved and well established.

5. *The aim of individual character formation is to become tov (or Christlike) in all relationships.* That means Christlike in small groups and congregational settings. Christlike in the family. Christlike at work. And Christlike in social settings. Wherever the individual goes, Christlikeness should be evident (Psalm 23:6).

CULTIVATE CONGREGATIONAL CHARACTER

The leadership at New Hope Church in Portland, Oregon, realized that the core of the church's mission had to be transformed toward character formation. They asked the same question that the leaders at Oak Hills had asked: What type of church do we want to be? That led to a brief statement of the church's mission: "Follow Jesus and share his love."

The leaders created a new articulation of values, such as "grace, change, people, Scripture, celebration, and justice." They pared back their theological statements to the essentials and used these touchstones to reshape their mission and every activity in the church that mattered.

A pastor at another church tweeted a great story, describing the formation of tov character in a church that's striving to look like Jesus:

Yesterday I spoke to a senior adult who recently visited our church. She's confined to a wheelchair, so I asked about her current mobility. She said, "I have a ramp, but I'm waiting to get it installed by city services."

"How long have you been waiting?" I asked.

"Eighteen months."

"Are you serious? Eighteen months??" I couldn't believe it.

She said that COVID made things worse, but really long waits are typical in that world. She went on to tell me that most of her family passed away years ago and she has only one friend in Austin.

"How can we help?" I asked.

She said, "Maybe you could put in a good word for me with city services?"

"Could we just come over to your house with a group of handy people from our church and install it?" I asked.

After a long pause, I could hear her choking back tears as she said, "You would do that?"

"Of course!" I said. "That's what the family of God is all about."

She replied, "I haven't had a family in a very long time. I think God knew how badly I needed one and that's why he sent me to your church."

This is why, despite all its issues, I can't leave [the] local church. We're going to be able to install a ramp, pull-up bars, and other mobility items at her home. We're also working on getting her a large-print Bible (her eyesight is fading), a better solution for mail (she can't get to her communal mailbox) and setting up a visiting schedule. I'm still convinced that there is nothing like the local church when it's healthy, inclusive, justice-driven and Jesus-centered.[17]

He later added a follow-up tweet:

Y'all are saying such kind things in the replies, but I want to make something clear: This is not about me. This is just how our church family operates. Restore members have been DM-ing me all day offering time and money to help her after reading this. I love our folks so much.[18]

Here's the kick in the shins: Character formation is much easier to get excited about than it is to develop and assess, whether in individuals, congregations, or institutions.

Follow Jesus.

Act with mercy.

Love God.

Pursue the Kingdom.

Love your neighbor.

Love your enemies.

Do to others what you want done to you.

It isn't enough to desire these virtues, or even to work on them ourselves. We must make these part of the culture in our churches. We must form these virtues into an energizing, nutrient-forming presence *in the soil* of our churches.

We must challenge ourselves and one another to *live out* the Ten Commandments; to *live out* the prophet's vision in Micah 6:8 (justice, kindness, humility); to *live out* the Sermon on the Mount's incredible picture of Kingdom life; to *live out* Paul's vision of life in the Spirit; to *live out* the love-infused life described by the apostle John in 1 John. Do the words *love, godliness, justice,* and *tov* describe what we are like?

TWO QUESTIONS

In the aftermath of so many revelations about senior pastors who have combined great talent with a failure of character, many people wonder about two issues: (1) "How can a person of such talent for Christian ministry do such immoral deeds?" and (2) "How was the abusive behavior allowed to become a pattern? Did anyone know? And if so, why didn't they do anything about it?"

It's the "Did anyone know?" question that unsettles us. Unfortunately, toxic, narcissistic leaders are motivated to hide their intentions and actions. In most churches we have read about and heard about and experienced firsthand, when a leader is accused, most people in the church (1) defend the pastor, (2) believe the pastor would never do such things, and (3) double down and turn against those who have lodged complaints against the pastor. In most cases where wrongdoing eventually was revealed, no one knew because the pastor made it very, very difficult for anything to be made known. Anyone who attempted to bring something to light was abused or silenced or disciplined or discredited so that others wouldn't believe the allegations. In simple terms, it's not only difficult to discover or identify the toxicity, it can be socially and personally dangerous to make it known.

The answer to the first question is both obvious and inexplicable: Yes, the same person can be both talented and lacking in character. Remember the war between the flesh and the Spirit, and the reality of sin and toxicity as systemic agents in human sinfulness. For the inexplicable part, we offer the incisive words of philosopher Martha Nussbaum:

> All my case studies . . . will document a particular type of
> deformed pride—the pride of people who think that their
> ability to dazzle others puts them above society's rules and
> even laws. . . . These distinguished artists show us something
> profoundly sad about human beings: that deep and subtle
> insight, and the ability to illuminate our lives in areas of
> the most profound human importance, can coexist with a
> warped, narcissistic, and utterly compassionless character.[19]

She's right, unfortunately. The same person can have wonderful and effective talent on the platform, and yet when no one is looking, act out of a corrupt character. That explains, in part, how Christians with great talent and impact can do such disgusting deeds.

As for the second question, we repeatedly observed the existence of "retainers," those who knew of abuses but assisted in maintaining the abuser's narrative, power, status, and platform persona. So, yes, almost always others know and yet allow it to happen. They are part of the problem of toxicity.

THE PROBLEM OF COMPLICITY

Wherever toxic leaders are found, you will also find enablers. Speaker and author Tiffany Bluhm, a survivor of abuse who has described toxic church cultures, highlights the role of accomplices and their complicity in a leader's abusive behavior:

> An offender often has accomplices—men and women who
> will do anything for him. They will excuse his behavior
> and drop everything to meet his whims. If they've made it
> into his inner circle and serve as gatekeepers to those on
> the outside, then they are likely the ones to do his bidding.
> They have proximity to power, privilege dependent on his

position, and they enable his abusive behavior with their
undying support and willingness to execute his plans. . . .
    His loyal puppets wear an invisible badge of honor. . . .
They may be the ones . . . with a message to deliver that
he doesn't care to deliver himself. They ensure things are
done his way. It doesn't matter if they exhibit high-caliber
character; it matters only that he can trust them.[20]

The accomplices become an abuser's frontline defense. And it's
not only men defending men in cultures that are too often sexualized
and harassing. Women also defend the offenders, thus re-wounding
the abused. Again, Tiffany Bluhm:

Nothing singes the skin more than other women—who
may have been considered friends and who were steeped
in the same sexualized culture together—who decimate
the character of a silence breaker and dismiss the actions
of a predator in an attempt to protect their positions.[21]

But you may wonder, as we have many times, why don't people
speak up or speak out? A pastor friend of ours pointed to the reasons
he has observed, which align with other examples we have seen.

1. Fear of losing a job, a career, a dream vocation.
2. Fear of being abused in turn.
3. Denial: Celebrity pastors can't be wrong; the other person
   deserved it.
4. Status enhancement of being on the celebrity pastor's good side.
5. Fear that others will not believe bad reports: victimization,
   gaslighting.
6. Belief that calling out the pastor will damage the image of the
   church.[22]

A seventh reason why many don't speak up is called betrayal
blindness, which describes a person's decision to forget, ignore,

overlook, or remain unaware of an act of betrayal. As first identified by psychology professor Jennifer Freyd,

> Betrayal trauma occurs when the people or institutions on which a person depends for survival significantly violate that person's trust or well-being: Childhood physical, emotional, or sexual abuse perpetrated by a caregiver are examples of betrayal trauma. . . . Victims, perpetrators, and witnesses may display betrayal blindness in order to preserve relationships, institutions, and social systems upon which they depend.[23]

Betrayal blindness can often occur when the abusive leader is a family figure, a father figure, or a spiritual mentor. When an authority figure does something that betrays the way of Christ, some people may choose not to believe it. Why? Because once it has been

---

Stockholm Syndrome may also help to explain why people don't speak up and challenge toxicities in the church. Here's how an article in *Psychology Today* about Stockholm Syndrome in the workplace explained it:

Stockholm Syndrome refers to the psychological phenomenon often observed in hostage situations where the hostages start to identify with (and sympathize with) their captor, even though mistreated. The captor controls the life source (food, water, shelter, etc.) of the captive, and punishment/reward is received from the same source: the captor.

Because so much of our self-worth in modern times is defined and derived by work, we are at risk for experiencing Corporate Stockholm Syndrome when put into a certain work environment for long enough. Corporate Stockholm Syndrome can be defined as employees of a business beginning to identify with—and being deeply loyal to—an employer who mistreats them (defined in this situation as verbal abuse, demanding overly long hours, and generally ignoring the well-being and emotional needs of the employee). As with the captor/captive dynamic, the employer is certainly in control of the employee's fate (they sign the much-needed paycheck and generally can terminate employment at any time).[24]

admitted, it must be experienced as betrayal—which can be unimaginably painful for the betrayed.

Character matters, not only with a senior pastor or teaching pastor, but with everyone around him or her. We taint our own character if we refuse to speak up when speaking up is the right thing to do.

GIVE TOV SPACE TO FLOURISH

Becoming a Christian doesn't automatically make someone act like Jesus. Nor does it promise that the senior leaders in your church will be uber-godly or that the pastors will be tov-er than Good King Wenceslas.

Just the other day, I heard a pastor say, "I don't *do* empathy."
Cringe!

A friend of mine who works with stressful church situations wrote to me (Scot): "I'm so disheartened with the church right now. The power and sexual abuse and dysfunction are inconceivable to me if the Spirit really indwells believers."

Right now in the North American church, we are experiencing the fruit of the kind of soil we have cultivated over the past two generations. Instead of developing godly character, we have cultivated

> It is personal ambition that drives the machinery of "success" in the church context, which is what comes out in the many dimensions of character failure that now are all too familiar.
>
> DALLAS WILLARD, FOREWORD TO *RENOVATION OF THE CHURCH*

leadership skills and talent. Nothing will change until we remove the toxins from the soil and give tov room to flourish. It will take power (see the next chapter), but only power that is tightly linked to tov character will transform a church culture into a tov culture.

Warm Up

1. For you:

   a. Do your habitual actions reveal that you value *character* or *talent* more highly? Explain.

   b. Describe a few recent examples from your life that would corroborate your answer above.

   c. In what ways have you been affected by leaders whose talent outpaced their character?

   d. Ask those who know you well whether you value character or talent more highly. What do they say? Why would they say they gave this answer?

   e. On which rung of the "character ladder" (pages 36–37) do you see yourself? Explain. What does this say about your own character development?

2. For your organization:

   a. Do your church's or organization's habitual actions reveal that it more highly values *character* or *talent*? Explain.

   b. Describe a few recent examples from the life of your church or organization that would corroborate your answer above.

   c. Ask those who are familiar with your church or organization whether it values *character* or *talent* more highly. What do they say? Why would they say they gave this answer?

   d. On which rung of the "character ladder" (pages 36–37) do you see your church or organization? Explain. What does this say about the cultural character of your church or organization?

Get Some Insight

1. Because effective character development requires accurate self-knowledge, spend some time with a few of the following assessment tools. We have organized these resources into three categories:

personality inventories; strengths and weaknesses assessments; cultural awareness tools. Some of the following links provide free access to helpful tools; others will connect you to a for-profit organization that offers an assessment tool. These tools can be used individually but are better processed in community, whether with staff, elders, or a circle of community around you.

- Personality inventories
    - Myers-Briggs Type Indicator: https://www.mbtionline.com/?msclkid=0e30f9fa28211f149e149b0fb634fb5b
    - Enneagram Personality Test: bestenneagramtest.com
    - Taylor Protocols Core Values Index: https://www.taylor protocols.com/index

- Strengths and weaknesses assessments
    - VIA Character Strengths Survey: https://www.viacharacter.org/account/register
    - CliftonStrengths Assessment: https://www.gallup.com/cliftonstrengths/en/252137/home.aspx
    - Marvin Oxenham's Virtue Education: https://virtueducation.net/

- Cultural awareness tools
    - Intercultural Development Inventory: https://idiinventory.com/
    - Cultural Intelligence Center: https://culturalq.com/

What did you learn about yourself through these resources?

2. It's one thing to know yourself; it's another thing to know how well you're cooperating with the Holy Spirit to form Christlike character in yourself and in your church or organization. Answer the following questions as honestly as you can—first for yourself and then for your church or organization.

a. Am I non-covetous?
   Are we non-covetous?
b. Am I demonstrating humility before God?
   Are we demonstrating humility before God?
c. Am I walking in the surpassing righteousness of Jesus?
   Are we walking in the surpassing righteousness of Jesus?
d. Am I loving?
   Are we loving?
e. Am I godly, just, and tov?
   Are we godly, just, and tov?
f. Am I Christlike?
   Are we Christlike?

As I was writing the questions for the previous section, I received a letter from a church leader telling me that his church, after a collision of powers between pastors on different campuses, had requested and received the resignation of its current lead pastor—*because of a lack of character*. I have heard enough stories from people I trust in that church to know that they hired the man based on his talent, charisma, and persuasiveness. He also exuded power and confidence. The pastor they got, sadly but predictably, was a man of ambition driven to succeed by measuring numbers, not a man of tov character.

Toxins will filter in and through an entire church community. If a toxic pastor leads a culture transformation effort, new toxins will flourish among the old ones. Not every accusation, allegation, or tweet fairly or accurately describes a situation, of course, but in the last three years, our inboxes have exploded with stories of power abuse by pastors and staff members who lack Christian character.

Character matters more than anything else.

We must develop tov character in our churches and Christian organizations. And we must give men and women with proven character the opportunity to lead.

Do the Hard Work

1. How well have you learned the virtues of the faith? How well do you practice them? Spend some unhurried time with each of the following five biblical paths to teaching the virtuous life. Each pathway can be

considered an on-ramp to teaching character. How well do you know each of these pathways? How well do you consciously strive to put them into practice? In what areas do you struggle the most?

a. The Ten Commandments (Exodus 20:1-17; Deuteronomy 5:6-21)
b. The ethical categories of the prophets (especially Micah 6:8)
c. The Sermon on the Mount (Matthew 5:1-7:29; Luke 6:20-49)
d. Life in the Spirit (Romans 5-8; Galatians 5:16-26)
e. Master categories: love, godliness, justice, tov

2. Spend additional prayerful time asking yourself how well your church or organization lives out these virtues. How well does the staff know these pathways? How well do volunteers, members, or regular attenders know these pathways? How could your church or organization help its people know them better and live them out more effectively?

3. Church culture transformation begins with personal, individual transformation.

a. What spiritual formation programs do you use to help develop godly character?
b. How does the progress of your own spiritual formation affect the well-being of your church or organization?
c. Where could you best use a mentor to help you in your personal spiritual formation? What would it take for you to become an effective mentor to someone else who needs help in personal spiritual formation?
d. Why is it important in a mentoring relationship to avoid coercive conversations, demands, and any kind of secretive "discernment" revelations? How do you avoid these things?
e. How Christlike do you think you have grown by this point in your spiritual formation? Give it a number, from 1 (not at all) to 10 (perfect). What are you doing well? Where are you struggling? What help do you think you need? Where can you get this help? Will you commit to getting the help you need? Explain.

f. Look again at the acts of the flesh listed in Galatians 5:19-21: "sexual immorality, impurity and debauchery; idolatry and witchcraft; hatred, discord, jealousy, fits of rage, selfish ambition, dissensions, factions and envy; drunkenness, orgies, and the like." Which of these do you find obvious in yourself? Would those close to you agree? What would growth and repentance look like for you in this area?

4

PRACTICE TOV POWER

PEOPLE HAVE POWER. Pastors have power. Denominational leaders have power. Leaders of Christian organizations have power. How these leaders use their power determines whether their culture becomes tov or toxic.

Culture transformation occurs *only through those with the power to make it happen.* How they use that power exposes their character. Do they use power the way Jesus did or like "the rulers of the Gentiles" he mentions in Matthew 20:25, who "lord it over" the people and "exercise authority over them"?

In the months after *A Church Called Tov* appeared, we received one story after another from people who had suffered power abuse in the church. Though we heard some accounts about sexual abuse, nearly all the stories concerned the abuse of power. Those who write to us often ask, "What can we do to transform the toxic culture in our church?" Before we proceed with answering that question, we want to share three important observations we have learned from pastors:

1. Transforming a culture requires power.
2. No culture can be transformed without access to power.
3. Though power can be dangerous, it is *not* inherently evil.

WHAT IS POWER?

With an eye on power abusers at every turn, we want to emphasize that power can be a force for *goodness* (tov) if tov people are the ones exercising power. So maybe we first should ask, *Where does power reside?*

Power is within you—in your mind, your heart, and your will. As humans, we have power because we are made in the image of the omnipotent God. To be human is to be given the gift and privilege of power. As humans, we each have a voice, we are in relationships with others, and therefore we are empowered to be agents of influence in our world. We also have the power of silence, emotional power, physical power (or lack of it), knowledge power, the power of absence, economic power, spiritual power, and cultural power. We enact power, and we experience power.[1]

In our communities, there is economic power, social power, and political power. There is the power of words, the power of culture, and the power of complicity. There is spiritual power and relational power. And there is systemic power, the power of society to coerce, constrain, and control.

> *Merriam-Webster* includes these definitions of *power*:
> 1. the ability to act or produce an effect
> 2. possession of control, authority, or influence over others
> 3. physical might, mental or moral efficacy, political control or influence[2]

What, then, is power? As we will use it in the following pages, power is *the capacity to influence people, including empowering others to do what they need to do to influence others*. That capacity may be God-given or it may be seized by a power-hungry person. Power may be derived from position, skill, or money. *Something* gives a person the capacity to influence others and shape a culture.

No one is more tempted to abuse power than someone who is zealous for transforming a culture or changing a group. Because people exercise power according to their character, people with tov character will exercise power in a tov manner.

The worst corruption of power is a corrupt pastor who purports to represent God to others. We rightly call this corruption of power *spiritual abuse*. Let us say it once more: *Those most passionate about transforming a culture will be tempted to engage in spiritual abuse.* Here's why: Passion naturally drives people toward their goals. Passion also drives people to knock down whatever stands in the way of their goals. When passion drives a pastor or other transformation agent who has some power, it can cause that person to run roughshod over people in the organization who are seen as not cooperating, who ask too many questions, or who simply oppose what the transformation agent is passionately pursuing.

POWER AND SPIRITUAL ABUSE

A leading agent in culture transformation has enough power to influence people, which opens the potential for spiritual abuse if the power is used badly. Coercive power is always abusive. When it is wielded by church leadership—individual or collective—it is classified as spiritual abuse.

Lisa Oakley and Justin Humphreys, two experts in the United Kingdom, have worked for years on defining spiritual abuse. We have reformatted their definition here:

Spiritual abuse is a form of emotional and psychological abuse characterized by a systematic pattern of coercive and controlling behavior in a religious context. Spiritual abuse can have a deeply damaging impact on those who experience it. This abuse may include:

- manipulation and exploitation
- enforced accountability
- censorship of decision making
- requirements for secrecy and silence
- coercion to conform [inability to ask questions]

- control through the use of sacred texts or teaching
- requirement of obedience to the abuser
- the suggestion that the abuser has a "divine" position
- isolation as a means of punishment
- superiority and elitism[3]

We could spend pages discussing this insightful definition, but drawing out a few central ideas will suffice. Spiritual abuse occurs in an asymmetrical spiritual relationship—that is, when one person (such as a pastor, Bible teacher, or favorite spiritual author) has more power than another. Spiritual abuse is an experienced reality, perceived and articulated by the one with less power. In many cases, spiritual abusers are unaware of what they are doing and would explain the experience in a very different way. But that doesn't mean what they're doing is not spiritual abuse! If what has been said or done is perceived by the recipient as coercive, controlling, manipulative, or exploitative, the elements of spiritual abuse are present, regardless of awareness or intent. But in most cases, spiritual abuse occurs in a *pattern* of similar behavior by one with spiritual power over another with less or no power. It rarely happens only once.

Please note: In the current cultural climate, spiritual abuse can be an easy accusation from someone who simply doesn't like the leader's or group's decisions. For the accusation to be accurate and potentially redemptive, we must understand what spiritual abuse is and have the skill and discernment to diagnose it. Spiritual abuse is most recognizable when the person in a position of spiritual power has a habit or exhibits a pattern of harming others.

Mature Christian leaders don't abuse others spiritually. Those who do must reform their understanding and use of power. In the "Getting to Work" section at the end of the chapter, we will see how Janet Hagberg's discussion of six stages of personal power in organizations can become a mirror for self-examination by agents of transformation.[4]

"THE KINGDOM OF GOD . . . IS A NEIGHBORHOOD"

While working on this book, I (Laura) formed a habit of watching episodes of *Mister Rogers' Neighborhood*.[5] I initially wanted to absorb Mr. Rogers' manner of teaching and connecting with young children as I prepared for my second year of teaching kindergarten. Though I certainly discovered profound practices to emulate, what I experienced in those thirty-minute interludes became moments of holiness. I found myself smiling at Mr. Rogers through the television screen and reveling in his kindness, his tov.

I nestled into my couch, beagle in my lap and coffee in hand, and breathed in the stillness and peace of Mr. Rogers' gentle, unhurried rhythms. He ministered to me in ways that were holy—and wholly unexpected—during a particularly painful summer. To borrow the words of writer Chris Buczinsky, I felt that Mr. Rogers was my pastor and the neighborhood he created was my church.[6] I watched this remarkably famous yet humble man use his extraordinary, far-reaching power *for* other people and ultimately *for* tov. *Power* is not a word we often connect with Mr. Rogers. (Do we ever?) But the very *absence* of evident power in Mr. Rogers reveals how artfully he wielded its graces.

> The very absence of evident power in Mr. Rogers reveals how artfully he wielded its graces.

In this book we have different ways of analyzing power, breaking it down into four principal uses. We scale these from toxic to tov.

The single most important practice in transforming a church culture is a Christlike exercise of power. The single biggest danger is misusing power. Without power, transformation won't happen; with power comes the temptation to abuse it. So let's make sure we get the power equation right.

POWER *OVER*

The first toxic use of power is domination—using strategic *power over* someone or *power over* an organization. Unfortunately, powerful people often *power over* others to accomplish their plans.[7] They manipulate and coerce and put people in positions where resistance means getting fired, reassigned, or humiliated. These are habits of the flesh, not the fruit of the Spirit. What, then, does *power over* look like?

1. *Power over turns other people into something less than human.* The dominated ones are turned into things to be manipulated. They become something less than real.
2. *The ones who power over consider themselves superior to others.* Abusive people consider themselves to be God's agents with some important agenda, as if they have inside information on the divine will. Their will is perceived as God's will. They stand above the rules that apply to everyone else.
3. *Power-over leaders tell the clear truth only to trusted insiders.* They lie to everyone else, who they believe "don't need to know" what's not good for them.
4. *Power-over leaders allow their corrupted pride to rule their relationships with others.* It's all about them. They see only what they can get from other people.
5. *People who power over are almost always people of unusual talent.*
6. *Males powering over females is systemic.*

Though men often don't perceive it (or won't admit it), women feel the *powering-over* dynamic in their bones. It only takes a man closing his office door with a woman subordinate to trigger the abused and activate her alarm bells. Many men don't even notice such things. Because the culture in most churches was created by men in positions of authority and influence, the male-centeredness remains as invisible to them as water to a guppy. Ask an introvert whether most church cultures are sensitive to introverts (especially on Sunday mornings), and you'll likely hear a quiet but firm *no*. Ask a woman whether church culture is sensitive to women, and you'll hear a louder and firmer *no*. Church cultures are notoriously unsafe for a woman's voice.

It's no surprise that the apostle Paul connects power to spirit-world principalities, to evil, and to the demonic realm. Notice these words from Ephesians 6:12:

> For our struggle is not against flesh and blood, but against the rulers, against the authorities, against the powers of this dark world and against the spiritual forces of evil in the heavenly realms.

Get ready to ask yourself about these items as you proceed through the transformation process. Ask this simple question to those around you who can safely be honest with you: "Am I abusing my power?"

Because it can be so tempting to abuse power without necessarily being aware of doing so, we want to quote at length Christian counselor Diane Langberg's examples of power abuse. As you read each one, we encourage you to ask yourself honestly, "Is this me?"

- Any time we use power to damage or use a person in a way that dishonors God, we fail in our handling of the gift he has given us.
- Any time we use power to feed or elevate ourselves, we fail in our care of the gift. Our power is to be governed by the Word of God and the Spirit of God.
- Any use of power that is not subject to the Word of God is a wrong use.
- Any use of power that is based on self-deception—when we have told ourselves that what God calls evil is instead good—is a wrong use. Remember that Adam and Eve, made in God's likeness, sought to be like him by eating what he had forbidden. The exercise of power in their choice to "be like God" required disobedience to God. It was therefore a wrong use of power.
- The exercise of the power of position to drive ministry workers into the ground "for the sake of the gospel" is a wrong use of power.

- Using emotional and verbal power to achieve our own glory, when God says he will share his glory with no one, is a wrong use of power.
- The power of success or financial knowledge used to achieve ministry ends, without integrity, is a wrong use of power.
- Using theological knowledge to manipulate people to achieve our own ends is a wrong use of power.
- Exploiting our position in the home or the church to get our own way, serve our own ends, crush others, silence others, and frighten others, is a wrong use of power.
- Using our influence or our reputation to get others to further our own ends is a wrong use of power.[8]

Remember, no one needs power more than the one who wants to transform a culture. But these instances of using power over others to get what we want is not Christlike.

The Way of Christ

At this point, we enter the radical theory of power taught by Jesus. The true exercise of power is to share it, use it for the sake of others, and empower others. Because humans are inherently sinful—imbued with what theologians call original sin—and are never *not* sinful, power must be checked by others exercising similar power (as in the separation of powers in the US government). Granting any human being ultimate power has but two possible outcomes: *tyranny* or *God-ness.*

Because only God is completely tov, and because no human is utterly tov except Jesus, every human endowed with ultimate power becomes a tyrant. Of course, all this operates on a spectrum. A tov leader will form a tov culture.

Sadly, very few are like Mr. Rogers—inclined toward tov. That's why it's healthy for us when power is dispersed and distributed. The next three uses of power we'll outline represent the revolutionary understanding of power in the Christian faith.

Theologian Hans-Ruedi Weber summarized this Christian

revolution: "Jesus transforms the love of power into the power of love."[9] Many have described the biblical approach to power using the term "servant leadership," but a better approach is to turn away from leadership manuals and learn to gaze into the face of Jesus. There we will see the all-powerful Lion of Judah, the risen Lamb who was slain. It is the slain Lamb who conquers the world.

POWER *WITH*

One of the best statements we've seen about power comes from Anne-Marie Slaughter: "Power shared is not the same as power delegated. It is shared within the give and take of a human relationship."[10] Some leaders think that by delegating responsibilities they are sharing power; but most likely they are not. They retain the power while assigning to others the tasks they don't want to do themselves.

Sharing power, or what we call *power with*, transcends delegation. In *power with*, feedback flows in both directions. Those "under you" know they are trusted, that they can express what they think needs to change, and that you, the leader, are as accountable to them as they are to you.

In a church, tov power is shared power. It is God's power operating with others. It is the power of a group united under the same Lord Jesus, empowered by the same Holy Spirit to manifest spiritual fruit and exercise gifts. It is the power of a congregation inspired to follow the same mission. Tov cultures form when everyone knows they are invited to the table, when everyone participates, and when everyone contributes what he or she is gifted and called to contribute. Power shared, or *power with*, happens when

> Those who have sipped from the cup of power are seldom content with other brews.
>
> MICHAEL KNOX BERAN, *WASPS*

those who have power divest themselves and share that power with others. *Power with* is not the *absence* of power; it is the *distribution* of power. Challenging as it can be to *power with*, Christ calls us to surrender power so that God's work may be accomplished by the many.

Of course, it takes plenty of uncoerced time for trust to form in a culture. Most of all, it requires humility for those in power to step aside, step down, or step back to allow others to exercise their gifts for the good of all.

The apostle Paul had a vision for spiritual gifts as *power with*. When every part of the body of Christ does what it does without desiring to do what other parts do, the whole body works well. Power needs to be shared. It will be shared when the key leaders and coalition members make it clear that they have committed themselves to forming a congregation-wide consensus for culture transformation.

The bright signal of *power with* is the authentic use of the word *we*. Not *we* when it means that many are not included. Rather, *we* as in, "We are proposing this and we need your feedback, because your feedback contributes to our vision." As in authentic, mutual co-pastoring. This sense of sharing power avoids deceit and pretense. *We* must genuinely mean sharing *power with*.

> The extra time it takes to run an idea by others or ensure that the right people are in the loop is actually time spent weaving a web of inclusion and accountability.
>
> ANNE-MARIE SLAUGHTER, *RENEWAL*

The *Mister Rogers' Neighborhood* episodes that mesmerized me (Laura), profound in their simplicity and overflowing in love, nearly brought me to tears. I watched Mr. Rogers put puzzles together and sing about feelings. He fed his fish and gently warned children to be careful jumping off tall things because people cannot fly like owls can.[11] He explained what buckets are and how we use them.[12] In the character of Daniel Tiger, he worried about being born a mistake.[13] Nothing was rushed; nothing a child asked or needed reassurance about was considered unimportant. He had unprecedented power to influence children and families, and he seemed to use every bit of it, every minute of every show, for love and goodness.

"You are my friend. You are special to me," he sang as I watched one morning. And then, before ending the episode and exiting through the familiar front door of the set, he explained: "When you like somebody, you want to share the things that you like with that person. I guess that's why I want to share so much with you. You make each day a special day by just being yourself. There's only one person in this world like you. People can like you just the way you are."[14]

This *power-with* approach of Mr. Rogers needs to penetrate to the depths of the transformation process. Conversations with others in the congregation, or even the key leaders' conversations with others as they form a coalition around the transformation vision, must not only convey *power with* but also genuinely share power by incorporating others into the process. The goal is what many call *buy-in* or *ownership*. Workplace gurus Gary Chapman, Paul White, and Harold Myra make the all-too-obvious but all-too-uncommonly-experienced observation that in the workplace, "people thrive when they feel *appreciated* by their supervisors and colleagues."[15] Beware the boss who refuses to offer words of affirmation! Deep and abiding transformation can occur only when leaders share power, affirm the contributions of others, own a group vision, and surrender their egos to the work of God.

A solemn reminder: Power is the single biggest temptation for those swept up into a vision of something better. One potent way to break down that temptation is to constantly work at sharing power with others.

POWER *FOR*

Power is not a zero-sum game. It is not quantifiable, as if, say, we have one hundred pounds of power, so if one person has sixty pounds, only forty pounds of power are left. That's not how the power of God (or the Spirit, or the congregation of grace) works.

When people use their power to empower others, they unleash the power of the Spirit—and God's power at work in us is both infinite and distributable. Because God's power is limitless, it can be compounded once unleashed. Agents of transformation who share power distribute it, and those agents who empower others give them *double* the power.

Notice how Jesus talks about power. In Mark 10:35-45 we read about two brothers who want power. They ask if they can have the power seats next to Jesus in the Kingdom of God. Jesus rebukes them, saying that they don't know what they're asking. And then Jesus gets to a brilliant expression about *power for*:

> You know that those who are regarded as rulers of the
> Gentiles lord it over them, and their high officials exercise
> authority over them. Not so with you. Instead, whoever
> wants to become great among you must be your servant, and
> whoever wants to be first must be slave of all. For even the
> Son of Man did not come to be served, but to serve, and to
> give his life as a ransom for many.
>
> MARK 10:42-45

Lording it over and exercising authority are examples of *power over*, but that is not the Jesus way: "Not so with you," he says. Rather, he measures greatness by those who choose to become "servants" and "slaves." Think about it: The entire life of a servant and a slave (all day, every day) is lived wholly *for someone else*. Jesus then teaches that *he* is the perfect example: "For even the Son of Man did not come *to be served*"—that is, to exercise *power over*—"but to serve, and to give his life as a ransom for many."

Power he had.

Power over he could have exercised.

Jesus exemplified *power for* because he used his power *for others*, divesting himself so it could benefit others. He gave himself to redeem others from their sin and death.

Jesus-generated power is a power to liberate others, which explains why the Bible connects the word *power* with exorcisms, healings, and miracles. Jesus' power liberates, and where there is liberation, there is the power of Jesus. Luke tells us that Jesus was filled with the Spirit and the power of God (Luke 4:14), and that is why he stunned people: "All the people were amazed and said to each other, 'What words these are! With authority and power he gives orders to impure spirits and they come out!'" (Luke 4:36). The "power of the Lord" enabled Jesus to heal (Luke 5:17). The power of Jesus is the power to liberate people from sin, from sickness, and from social and systemic injustices.

Paul carried on the vision of *power for* when he wrote to the Philippians. Some in those house churches wanted *power over*, and Paul wanted them to see that the way of Jesus is the way of *power for*. He appealed to Jesus as the preeminent example.

Philippians 2:3-11 is one of the most beautiful passages in the entire Bible on the Christian use of power. Every church going through a transformation process would benefit if the leaders memorized these verses and recited them to each other weekly. When one of my pastor-students discussed a church transformation process, he reminded us that we all need to focus on "who we are becoming." This passage teaches us what we want to become, and the best word for it is *Christoformity*, or Christlikeness:

> Do nothing out of selfish ambition or vain conceit. Rather, in humility value others above yourselves, not looking to your own interests but each of you to the interests of the others.
>
> In your relationships with one another, have the same mindset as Christ Jesus:
>
> Who, being in very nature God,
>> did not consider equality with God something to be used
>>> to his own advantage;
> rather, he made himself nothing
>> by taking the very nature of a servant,
>> being made in human likeness.
> And being found in appearance as a man,
>> he humbled himself
>> by becoming obedient to death—
>>> even death on a cross!
>
> Therefore God exalted him to the highest place
>> and gave him the name that is above every name,

that at the name of Jesus every knee should bow,
   in heaven and on earth and under the earth,
and every tongue acknowledge that Jesus Christ is Lord,
   to the glory of God the Father.

PHILIPPIANS 2:3-11

Jesus accomplished redemption, the "ransom for many" of Mark 10:45, only by using his infinite power over all creation *for the sake of others.* That same power led him back to the right hand of the Father to exercise the same authority eternally. In the example set by Jesus, the way to greatness is the way of servanthood or slavery.

Back to Mr. Rogers. For three decades, led by the Spirit, Fred Rogers made children and adults feel special, valued, and important— via television, of course, but also in person. "I like you just the way you are," he told his audience daily on *Mister Rogers' Neighborhood,* and we believed him. Why? Because we trusted him. We trusted how special he made us feel. Journalist and author Tim Madigan remembers his first conversation with Mr. Rogers:

> In the first telephone call, at the end of an hour, a fairly long time for a celebrity to be talking to a reporter, . . . he said to me, "Tim, do you know what the most important thing in my life is right now? . . . [It's] speaking to [you] on the telephone."[16]

Is there anything more holy and honoring to another human being than to give them your very presence, your full attention, your time, and your care? Mr. Rogers wielded considerable power *for the sake of others,* so much so that we struggle to connect the man with power at all!

One of the most breathtakingly beautiful examples of *power for* that we've seen occurred in the village of Le Chambon-sur-Lignon, France, when German forces occupied it during World War II. Villagers, led by pastor André Trocmé and part-time pastor Édouard

Theis, used every bit of their influence to offer refuge in the village and save Jewish lives during the Holocaust. Theirs was a self-sacrifical and profound purpose: *to save human lives at the peril of their own.*[17]

Le Chambon's villagers, "under the guidance of a spiritual leader . . . were trying to act in accord with their consciences in the very middle of a bloody, hate-filled war."[18] The village leaders used their power for the sake of others. Day after day, agonizing conversation after conversation, they poured their character into the character of the entire community. Their actions testified to their firm dedication to human life, relief from suffering, and hope.

This village of three thousand people ultimately saved about five thousand Jewish refugees, using their power for the greatest of goodness and for the sake of strangers. Trocmé merits quite a description: "He kept discovering new things to do that would give substance to the words . . . 'Love one another.'"[19] We encourage you to read Le Chambon's tov-est of examples in Philip Hallie's *Lest Innocent Blood Be Shed: The Story of the Village of Le Chambon and How Goodness Happened There.*

We can't emphasize it enough: The biggest issue in toxic church cultures is abuse of power. One could call it the deadliest toxin in a church's soil. For a church culture to be transformed from toxic to tov, those with power must surrender that power by using it for goodness, by sharing it with others, and by using their own power for others.

Richard Foster discusses seven marks of spiritual power, what we call *power for*: love, humility, self-limitation, joy, vulnerability, submission, and freedom. In the individual, this kind of power leads to self-control; in the home, confidence; in a marriage, communication; in the church, faith; in the school, growth; and on the job, competence.[20] One could add a few others, subtract one or two, and still end up in the same place: This is the fruit that grows on tov trees that uses power for the sake of others. Transforming a culture for tov begins and ends with how power is used.

Let's turn now to the most radical vision of power in the entire
New Testament.

POWER *THROUGH*

To use one's power for another person's good and even glory is radical. But to have power and give it away, what we call *power through*,
goes beyond even *power with* and *power for*. We therefore want to
make a subtle distinction between *power with* and *power for* before
we consider *power through*.

You have power as a person, as a leader, as an agent for transformation. You can use that power *over* someone to accomplish what
you want. Or you can work *with* others and exercise *power with* in
a shared fashion. You can even go further in the direction of tov by
using your *power for* someone else's good.

This *power with* and *for* can be extended to someone else when
the power granted by God moves *through you* into another so they
can be transformed into an agent of tov for others. As Christians,
we know that whatever power we have is derivative and comes to us
from God. Listen to Jesus' promise that he will be with us as a resting,
divine presence:

> Therefore go and make disciples of all nations, baptizing
> them in the name of the Father and of the Son and of the
> Holy Spirit, and teaching them to obey everything I have
> commanded you. And surely *I am with you always*, to the
> very end of the age.
>
> MATTHEW 28:19-20 (ITALICS ADDED)

Jesus calls his apostles to join the mission to disciple the nations,
and in that mission he promises his presence. This is God's power in
Jesus moving through him into us. When Jesus sent out his disciples
for the first time, he spoke words they not only would remember, but
would also need again and again, for the rest of their lives, in pursuit
of their mission:

When they arrest you, do not worry about what to say
or how to say it. At that time you will be given what to
say, for it will not be you speaking, but the Spirit of your
Father speaking through you.

MATTHEW 10:19-20

Jesus promises God's presence to his disciples when they speak, so
that what they say will be "the Spirit of your Father speaking *through
you*." It is no stretch to see this as the distribution of power by the
one who chose not to *power over*, but to *power for* so that it became
power through.

Too many leaders see power as a zero-sum game: "If I have it,
you don't." But power for the vision of Jesus is unlimited, because
Jesus said, "*All* authority in heaven and on earth has been given to
me" (Matthew 28:18, italics added). Not *some*, but *all*. And he distributed power to his apostles when he sent them out in Matthew 10.
In verse 1, we read that he "gave them authority." The power and
authority that he himself displayed in Matthew 8 and 9 was given
to the disciples to extend the mission. Jesus said it this way: "As you
go, proclaim this message: 'The kingdom of heaven has come near.'
Heal the sick, raise the dead, cleanse those who have leprosy, drive
out demons" (Matthew 10:7-8).

This is the ultimate form of divine power: the release of God's
power *to* us and *through* us into others, so they can extend the mission of Jesus even further.

POWER AND YOU

You have power. How will you use it? Will you use it for yourself,
or will you use it for others and thereby become an agent of God's
power through you to others? The temptation to use *power over* will
accompany every thought, every decision, every conversation, and
every plan made by change agents.

It would be utopian to think that transformation agents, especially founding leaders in a church, will easily and simply divest

themselves of power. It would be great to imagine that everyone gets filled up with the Holy Ghost and it all goes swimmingly, sparklingly beautiful. But that isn't how it works, is it?

Leaders are transformation agents whose power becomes enculturated. Ponder the words of one major thinker about transformation:

> Founding leaders usually *impose* structure, systems, and processes based on their own beliefs and values. If the organization is successful, they [leader and structure, etc.] become shared and parts of the culture. And once those processes have become taken for granted, they become the elements of the culture that may be the hardest to change.[21]

When a church realizes its system has snapped and needs culture transformation, the designated transformation agent has power. The easiest way forward is to nuance the structures that exist, to decorate them with new colors and try to shift perceptions by using new terminology—but that will never transform the system. It will remain the same old toxic system, merely with new names, new leaders, and new ideas.

For real transformation to happen, the transformation agent must be a person with a new, tov character (or someone who is increasing in tov character), and the culture must be rebuilt with nutrients that will lead to tov fruit.

We believe power is the most important element in transforming culture. It is supremely important because it is the most robust, the most influential, and the most dangerous. Raw power morphs into Christian power when shaped by a tov character. So take careful note: The ideas in chapters 3 and 4 work *only* when they work together.

Warm Up

1. Reflect on the following statement (or better yet, have a conversation about it with a trusted colleague):

   No one is more tempted to abuse power than someone who is zealous for transforming a culture or changing a group.

2. Discuss the following statement with a small group of trusted colleagues:

   The worst corruptions of power are corrupt pastors representing God to others.

Get Some Insight

1. Read over the ten varieties of spiritual abuse identified by Lisa Oakley and Justin Humphreys on pages 61–62.

   a. Have you seen any of these behaviors in operation in your church or organization? If so, where? How often?
   b. If you recognize more than one of these behaviors in your church or organization, rank the ones you have identified, from most common to least common. What strategies could you and your colleagues begin using to eliminate these behaviors?
   c. Which of these behaviors are you most tempted to engage in? Explain.
   d. Think of the people you have seen who have been abused in any of these ten ways. What can you do to help these people? What can your church or organization do?

2. Janet Hagberg has identified six stages of power used by leaders.[22]
   These stages move from abusive (stage 1) to what we'd call tov
   (stage 6).

STAGE OF POWER	LEAD BY	INSPIRE	REQUIRE	MANAGE BY
Stage 1	Force	Fear	Blind obedience	Muscling
Stage 2	Rules	Dependency	Followers who need them	Maneuvering
Stage 3	Persuasion	A winning attitude	Loyalty	Monitoring
Stage 4	Modeling integrity	Hope	Consistency, honesty	Mentoring
Stage 5	Empowering others	Love and service	Self-acceptance, calling	Moseying
Stage 6	Wisdom	Peace	Anything-everything-nothing	Musing

a. Think honestly about your own leadership style. Which stage most
   closely represents you? Explain.
b. Think honestly about the leadership styles of leaders in your church
   or organization. Which stage most closely represents them? Explain.
c. If you are not at the sixth stage, what will it take for you to get there?
d. If the leaders in your church or organization are not at the sixth
   stage, what will it take for them to get here?

3. Julie Battilana and Tiziana Casciaro write, "Although power is essential
   to taking charge and driving change, it makes leaders vulnerable to two
   traps that can not only erode their own effectiveness but also undermine
   their team's. *Hubris*—the excessive pride and self-confidence that can
   come with power—causes people to greatly overestimate their own
   abilities, while *self-focus* makes them less attentive to subordinates,
   diminishing their ability to lead successfully."[23]

a. Describe the last time you overestimated your own abilities. Could
   hubris have had something to do with that? Explain.
b. Describe the last time you focused so much on self that you

diminished your ability to lead successfully. What happened? How could you have prevented it?

c. Think of the leaders in your church or organization. Is hubris or self-focus a problem? Explain.

4. Battilana and Casciaro give four tips for cultivating humility:

- Make it acceptable—even desirable—to say, "I don't know."
- Establish ways to obtain honest input.
- Create visible reminders that success is fleeting.
- Measure and reward humility.[24]

a. Which of these suggestions resonates most with you? Why?

b. Which of these suggestions, if implemented, would have the greatest potential to improve the culture at your church or organization? Why?

5. Battilana and Casciaro also give four tips for cultivating empathy:

- Immerse yourself in other people's jobs.
- Use storytelling to make things personal.
- Embed interdependence in organizational systems.
- Step out of your company and into the real world.[25]

a. Which of these suggestions resonates most with you? Why?

b. Which of these suggestions, if implemented, would have the greatest potential to improve the culture at your church or organization? Why?

Do the Hard Work

1. Review the six characteristics of leaders who use *power over* to get things done (page 64).

a. Do you see yourself in any of these characteristics? If so, which ones? Be honest.

b. Do any of the leaders in your church or organization struggle with any of these characteristics? If so, what can you do to helpfully address the problem with them?

2. Review Diane Langberg's ten examples of power abuse (pages 65–66).

a. Give yourself a test. Read the ten examples of power abuse and ask yourself, "Is this me?"

b. If you are a leader, ask those around you (who can safely be honest with you), "Am I abusing my power in any of these ten ways?"

3. Define for yourself the term *power with*. What does this term convey to you?

a. How is distributing power different from delegating?

b. If you are a leader, how do you distribute your power at your church or organization?

c. How "we" is your church or organization's culture?

d. How do you typically affirm the contributions of others?

e. How do members of your church or organization own the group's vision?

f. How do you surrender your ego to the work of God in your church or organization?

4. Define for yourself the term *power for*. What does this term convey to you?

a. In what practical ways do you live out the message of Mark 10:35-45 in your church or organization? In what ways do you struggle to live it out?

b. In what practical ways do the leaders of your church or organization live out the message of Mark 10:35-45? In what ways do they struggle to live it out?

c. How do you use your power to liberate others in your church or organization?

    d. How do the leaders in your church or organization use their power to liberate others?

    e. Meditate for a week on Philippians 2:3-11. How does this passage instruct you about your use of power in your church or organization? What would you have to change to more completely fulfill its message?

    f. Review Richard Foster's seven marks of spiritual power on page 73. Which of these marks do you believe you have a pretty good handle on? Which do you tend to struggle with? How can you improve this week on using your *power for* others?

5. Define for yourself the term *power through*. What does this term convey to you?

    a. How is the power granted to you by God moving through you to others, so they can be transformed into agents of tov for others?

    b. How can you use your *power for* so that it becomes *power through*?

    c. If you are in a church or organization that recognizes it needs transformation, how can you avoid nuancing existing structures—decorating them with new colors and trying to shift perceptions by using new terminology—and instead move toward the needed transformation?

    d. How does your character shape your use of power?

BECOME A
TOV EXAMPLE

ONE OF THE MOST MEMORABLE experiences in my (Laura's) teaching career was the year I first taught kindergarten. Being an example always matters, but especially so for kindergartners—and even more so during a pandemic. Instructing these kindergarteners provided an assortment of unprecedented teaching challenges, not the least of which was dual-platform instruction.

I taught a class of eighteen boys and girls (ten in person and eight remote). This meant incorporating a live video feed for all instruction and meeting the unique social-emotional needs of isolated children . . . kindergartners, remember. It also meant teaching phonics with a mask over my mouth and shouting so I could be heard by both remote students and those in the classroom.

"Imagine I am sticking out my tongue to make the *th* sound," I would explain while trying to show them. Comical? Without question, especially as they, too, stuck out their tongues behind their masks to make the *th* sound. We all shrugged our shoulders and hoped for the best.

At 10 a.m. on day one of kindergarten, my in-person students announced they had no more interest in Zooming with the children at home. I interrupted the live video instruction constantly during those first few days—for telephone calls, shoe-tying incidents, ants, flies, microscopic cuts (or more likely, "blood" that was actually red marker). On occasion, a student got stuck in the bathroom, pounding on the door about his predicament.

"I'll be right back!" I yelled to my remote students, running to the phone or to the bathroom or to the commotion in the back of the classroom over an unidentified insect.

"Do not kill living things!" the kindergartners would yell, which created even more diversion and more prolonged absence from remote students as we let the mangled creature go free outside. I would return, breathless, to the Zoom session, typically forgetting what I had been teaching prior to the latest classroom clamor.

Nevertheless, I needed to nurture our classroom culture. Never did I work so hard to embody a safe, loving environment for these children who were living through months of pandemic isolation. We slowly settled into a rhythm, the most important part of which became our morning meeting. Every day at 9 a.m., from August until our last day in June, my students and I began our day by singing, "Hello, Neighbor" to each other. And then we talked.

I asked a question of the day, and sometimes we discussed feelings and learned what mattered to each other. "You are important to me," I told them each day, attempting to emulate Mr. Rogers, "and I want to learn more about you." They seemed to revel in the attention.

My favorite days were birthdays. We took turns telling the birthday child one specific thing we loved about him or her. "I really like your shoes," someone would say. Or more often, "You should raise your hand more before you talk." No matter. They simply loved the routine, the constancy, the attention, the interaction, the dependable rhythm of being seen and known.

Day after day, week after week, month after month, we built together a culture of safety and love, where everyone was valued and included. All the while I—copying Mr. Rogers—tried to be an example of my own teaching. As time passed and trust formed, I often heard my students repeat my words to one another: "It doesn't have to be perfect, James! Just try your best! You're only in kindergarten!"

It humbled me and reminded me that children learn most by example. They wanted a reliable teacher who provided a safe classroom in which to learn and grow, and I wanted to be an example to them.

(Even if they never did properly learn the *th* sound.)

EMULATION AS EDUCATION FOR TRANSFORMATION

One pastor we consulted about transforming church cultures said over breakfast to me (Scot), "I realized I couldn't ask people to do what I was not already doing. Not just doing, but doing well."[1]

Sondra Wheeler, a professor who teaches future ministers how to nurture spirituality in others, said, "Because ministers will continually be preaching by behavior and teaching by example, they must also become certain kinds of people." She reminds us of the importance of character formation—that is, being "not only people who possess certain knowledge and techniques but also people whose character is shaped in particular ways."[2]

One of my students, Vic Copan, now also a professor deeply concerned with spiritual formation, studied the power of example in helping people grow to be more Christlike. In his book *Saint Paul as Spiritual Director*, he explains how discipling others can too easily degrade into a series of techniques. Vic counters techniques with the most important lesson for those who want to transform a church culture. He uses the image of a pastor as a spiritual director:

> It is my contention . . . that the total shape of the life of the
> director is a key factor—if not *the* key factor—in the success
> of spiritual direction; effectiveness in spiritual direction is
> not to be found primarily in technique, but in the character
> and lifestyle of the one providing the direction.[3]

More than ideas or techniques, the character of the role model matters most. The infamous adage "Do as I say, not as I do" was repeated to me a few times by some who ought to have known better. It gets the point exactly backwards. It should be, "Do as I do."

So let's back up to the transformation agents as they work for deep growth in the soil. We tell them that what they *do* matters more than what they *say*. Dave Ferguson, in an article about culture change, defines this step with two simple words: "Do it." He warns pastors, preachers, and teachers who are trying to lead culture change in their organizations, "You will be tempted to teach it or vision cast it. Please resist. Before you teach it, you need to do it yourself. . . . You will reproduce *not* what you teach, but what you *do*!"[4]

> The answer for Christian communities is that we should have Christian leaders who are characterized by the relational qualities that we want everyone else to copy.
> DOUGLAS CAMPBELL, *PAUL: AN APOSTLE'S JOURNEY*

Emulation is the first principle of formation and transformation. Children imitate parents and siblings, students emulate their teachers and peers. How did you learn to write? Throw and catch and bat? Relate to friends? Prepare for exams? Form successful habits at work? How did you learn to bake bread or make an omelet? You learned some things by reading or hearing, but mostly you learned by watching, by imitating, by emulating. More people learn how to do something by watching YouTube than by reading the instructions on the box.

The Bible and Emulation

God taught Israel to learn by emulation. Consider the Bible's original instruction for education. Please read these verses slowly, for they not only reveal the basis of Israel's education but the backbone of Israel's way of life:

> These are the commands, decrees and laws the LORD your
> God directed me to teach you to observe in the land that you
> are crossing the Jordan to possess, so that you, your children

and their children after them may fear the LORD your God
as long as you live by keeping all his decrees and commands
that I give you, and so that you may enjoy long life. Hear,
Israel, and be careful to obey so that it may go well with you
and that you may increase greatly in a land flowing with
milk and honey, just as the LORD, the God of your ancestors,
promised you.

Hear, O Israel: The LORD our God, the LORD is one. Love
the LORD your God with all your heart and with all your
soul and with all your strength. These commandments that
I give you today are to be on your hearts. Impress them on
your children. Talk about them when you sit at home and
when you walk along the road, when you lie down and when
you get up. Tie them as symbols on your hands and bind
them on your foreheads. Write them on the doorframes of
your houses and on your gates.
DEUTERONOMY 6:1-9

This is how Mary the mother of Jesus learned from her parents.
This is how Jesus learned from his parents. This is how Paul learned
from his parents. This is how John and James and Junia and Priscilla
. . . you get the point. This is how everyone learned in the ancient
world.

As Paul instructed the Philippians, "Whatever you have learned
or received or heard from me, or seen in me—put it into practice"
(Philippians 4:9). This theme of emulation goes deeper than "follow
me." Paul also wrote, "Follow my example, as I follow the example of
Christ" (1 Corinthians 11:1). Emulation is the first mode of *formation* and *transformation*.

Paul reminded Timothy of this very thing in words we may easily overlook: "As for you, continue in what you have learned and
have become convinced of, because you know those *from whom you
learned it*, and how *from infancy* you have known the Holy Scriptures"
(2 Timothy 3:14-15, italics added). Paul also said something similar at the beginning of his letter: "I am reminded of your sincere

faith, which first lived in your grandmother Lois and in your mother Eunice and, I am persuaded, now lives in you also" (2 Timothy 1:5). Timothy learned the faith through the example of his mother and grandmother. This explains why sociologists sometimes call our home life *primary* socialization, while what we learn from everyone else—teachers, friends, coworkers, what we read—is called *secondary* socialization.[5]

When Jesus called Simon Peter and his brother Andrew, and when he called James and John, the sons of Zebedee, he instructed them, "Come, follow me" (Matthew 4:19). Disciples of Jesus *followed* him (Matthew 4:22). We need to look beyond the simplicities that sometimes pop up around common words and phrases such as *disciple* and "follow Jesus" to realize that these were real people following a real Messiah. *Following* in this context means:

being with Jesus,
watching him,
listening to him,
being instructed by him,
doing what he said, and
doing what he did.

After Matthew finishes outlining Jesus' teaching, preaching, and healing ministries (Matthew 5–9), he says that Jesus "called his twelve disciples to him" and made them apostles by sending them out *to do what he had been doing*, because they had seen him doing those very things (Matthew 10:1-10). Followers of Jesus follow Jesus. Emulation is at the heart of formation.

> People will follow what they see before what they hear.

Though we can make too much of "What would Jesus do?" we can also make too little of it. We are called *Christians* (a diminutive of *Christ*) because we are to be "little Christs"— to emulate him. We are little Christs when we do and say what Jesus would do and say. Jesus is our first example, and those who follow Jesus are second examples. Which is why we cited the apostle Paul's words: "Follow my example, as I follow the example of Christ."

TRANSFORMATION BY EMULATION

We learn more by emulation than by information, which means exactly what the pastor told me at breakfast: Transformation will happen only through emulation. This means we need tov people to emulate. Our churches need more and more examples of Jesus. The greatest cultural transformation occurs when *a band of Christians* begins to walk in the way of Jesus so well that other people see Jesus in how the community of faith lives.

More particularly, the culture shift you want to see in your church *requires* people who are *already* doing what you want others to do, so that those you want to enlist in the culture shift *can see* what they are to do themselves. Let's ramp this up one level.

A pastor friend who is involved in an eight-year culture shift in a church described one of the most important realizations he and his people had: "Who we are *becoming* is more important than *where we are headed.*" Which is to say, it isn't just *what we do* but *who we are.*

It all comes down to *character.*

Let's dig in here a bit. In our churches we measure numbers. We assess success through quantitative measurements. We measure butts in seats, bills in plates, baptisms in water, and buildings on the rise.[6] When attendance grows, when the budget swells, when conversions increase, and when buildings take up space on our property, we see ourselves as doing the Lord's work well.

What we're saying instead is that we need to pivot. We need to measure *character formation* more than *number enhancements.* Why? The thing that matters most—pick the term you prefer—is spiritual formation, character development, Christlikeness, tov. Someone once said, "If you can't count what matters, then make what you can count matter." John Rosensteel, a former student of mine at Northern Seminary and now pastor of New Hope Church in Portland, Oregon, said it this way:

For most of my ministry career, I was taught to determine success through the matrix of business principles. I was told that healthy things grow. But I came to realize that numerical growth can be a misleading indicator of a flourishing church. There are some inherent tensions between selling out to attract crowds and a devotion to making disciples. Large, numerically growing churches can certainly flourish and make disciples. Yet that is not necessarily the case. Healthy things do grow, but the growth that matters is difficult to capture in a spreadsheet. It is difficult to track. It is slow, messy, and eludes simple measurements, but you know it when you see it.[7]

Instead of measuring tov character in our US churches, we chose to measure numbers. And it's killing us.

New Hope: Be the Example

As John Rosensteel began to pioneer a culture transformation at New Hope Church, he knew it had to begin with his own life. When a near heart attack woke him up, he began to get counseling. He and his wife also underwent marriage therapy. He formed a relationship with a spiritual director named Morris, who had burned out attempting a church culture transformation. Morris had then created a ministry called Soul Formation that nurtured pastors in the tensions of pastoring. He taught John to live in God's grace and unfading love.

Not only did John learn about himself, but he led New Hope into working with other churches and pastors. I know from experience the importance of the network of pastors in Portland for sustaining the health of those pastors and their churches. John candidly described the process he went through:

Through counseling, spiritual direction, involvement in an eighteen-month spiritual formation experience, and the support of brothers and sisters in our city, I began to heal and develop the internal infrastructure to pastor and lead from a place of health. Cracks of light began to emerge. Hope dawned.[8]

You cannot lead a transformation in your church without first leading one in your own soul.

From One Person to a Community

New Hope provided an example of both individual and congregational transformation. John Rosensteel and New Hope dug into their own stories and moved into transformation at both the personal and church level.

My (Scot's) favorite theologian, Dietrich Bonhoeffer, once said that "the church's word gains weight and power not through concepts *but by example.*"[9] He wrote those words to his best friend, Eberhard Bethge, while in prison in August 1944. Some eight years earlier, in a letter Bonhoeffer sent to his students as the danger of Hitler's rise to power became evident, he made a similar statement in an even more expansive way. Answering the question, What makes for a real church of Jesus Christ?, he wrote, "It is not the religious formula, dogma, that constitutes the church *but the practical doing of what has been commanded.*"[10]

The church is only fully the church when it lives in the way of Jesus; when through emulation of the Master himself, it is transformed. Emulation is not just a personal, individual thing but also a community vision.

Gander, Newfoundland, and September 11, 2001

For a beautiful example of emulation, of community, of welcoming visitors, we look to the town of Gander, Newfoundland, and its legacy after the attacks of September 11, 2001. Gander's story is wonderfully told in the Broadway production *Come from Away*, through which I (Laura) swallowed tears for the better part of ninety minutes as I marveled at the beauty of its community vision of love.

Gander, a tiny village located in the northeastern part of the island of Newfoundland in the Canadian province of Newfoundland and Labrador, hosts Gander International Airport, once an important refueling stop for transatlantic aircraft. When the United States closed its airspace immediately after the attacks on 9/11, Gander International Airport landed thirty-eight commercial aircraft and four military planes, with a combined total of nearly seven thousand passengers on board.[11]

What does a small community do when thousands of people suddenly and unexpectedly arrive on one of history's darkest days? What does it do with thousands of anxiety-ridden souls in the midst of a national crisis? This is what Gander did: "Without hesitation, the Newfoundlanders opened their homes to let them shower; their school gyms, community centers, and hotels to let them sleep and eat warm meals; and their hearts to the unknowns following a tragedy of such magnitude."[12] The community cared for animals in the cargo areas of grounded planes, and its people provided telephones to stranded passengers who wanted to talk to loved ones. They sat with mothers who anxiously awaited news from New York City about firefighter sons.

In this book, we focus on *why* Gander did what it did. What in its soil produced such healthy, beautiful acts of love? For "people did it without any instructions—it was something that really came naturally to our people and volunteers," Gander mayor Derm Flynn said. He and his wife, Diane, invited six of the stranded travelers to stay in their three-bedroom home after the planes were grounded. "Our house is always open," he said.[13]

Long before 9/11, a rich history of hospitality flourished in the soil of Gander, so much so that the town couldn't help but be hospitable. And the culture of hospitality spread.

The community never expected any attention when its people sprang into action, but two decades later, those events have completely shaped not only Gander, but also the world's perspective on the essential nature of embedded goodness.

Today, a piece of damaged steel sits on the floor in the lobby of Gander's town hall. The steel, a remnant from the debris of the World Trade Center in New York, is one of two pieces gifted to the town from the United States on the tenth anniversary of 9/11. The gift says thank you for the work that people from the town and surrounding area did for those passengers who found themselves stranded when American airspace shut down in the aftermath of the 9/11 attacks.[14] This mangled remnant from the south tower provides a town of great love a lasting opportunity to remember.

WORTHY OF EMULATION

It all begins with each of us increasingly becoming an example worthy of emulation. Since stories are the best way to teach emulation, we want to tell two.

It Begins with Each of Us

Author Shea Tuttle penned a delightfully poignant book about Fred Rogers called *Exactly as You Are: The Life and Faith of Mister Rogers.* She describes his ministry, which extended beyond the television screen to those who knew him. He didn't just say, "Go love people." He loved people. He first set an example.

Lisa Hamilton, who worked for Fred Rogers, was the beneficiary of one of his Holy Spirit–prompted actions, and she remembered it for the rest of her life. Tuttle describes Lisa's gratitude for her employer after the death of her young husband.

> Lisa . . . remembers Fred's presence at a very painful time in her life. She and her husband, Scott, were both thirty-one years old when they learned that he had cancer. During the eight months of Scott's illness, Fred regularly came to visit, and he would pray with Scott, Lisa, and their son, Teddy. . . .
>
> One morning, she [Lisa] woke up, still holding Scott's hand, to find that he had died.

"I was really panicky," Lisa said. "And the doorbell rang."

When she opened the door, she found Fred standing there. . . .

"I was praying," Fred said, "and I felt you needed some help."

"So, Fred Rogers is the person who called the funeral home," Lisa told me. "And he wept over Scott's body—the only person I remember weeping with me." . . .

Fred stayed in touch with her and Teddy for the rest of his life, sending cards or calling on Teddy's birthdays as X the Owl (Teddy's favorite puppet). . . .

Years later, Lisa found out . . . that though Fred had shared the news of Scott's death . . . with the staff, he never told them about his timely appearance at Lisa's door. But this didn't surprise Lisa. "He did a lot quietly," she said. "So, I feel that I am one of probably hundreds of people with stories like that."[15]

To return to the term *soil*, when Mr. Rogers committed himself to the soil of his own character, we witnessed the beautiful, healthy fruit that his neighborhood and his life produced. His example nourished many and encouraged countless others to live as he lived.

Parish for the Poor

Forty-five years ago, in partnership with a local Detroit church and three friends, the Reverend Tom Lumpkin founded and launched a ministry called the Manna Meal soup kitchen. For four decades, if you wandered by St. Peter's Episcopal Church any morning from 8 to 9 (except Thursdays and Sundays), you'd find Lumpkin serving breakfast and distributing lunches to Detroit's homeless population.

Lumpkin had a calling to serve the poor, a ministry begun not long after a four-year visit to postwar Europe in 1960.

"It was my first exposure to poverty," he said. "I was in Naples and saw people living in refrigerator boxes. I saw homeless people."[16] Lumpkin felt so moved by this exposure to extreme poverty that he responded radically, by measuring his food intake for the remainder of his time in seminary and eventually committing his life to the cause. One might describe his life as transformed by what he saw and experienced. Lumpkin himself became a model to emulate.

But first, ordained and back in the United States, Lumpkin served a nine-year stint in suburban ministry. He felt unsettled in such comfortable settings and felt called to serve those in poverty, much as he had witnessed in Europe. And this unsettled feeling—what we describe as a prompting of the Holy Spirit, a transformation of the soul—led to the opening of a hospitality home and soup kitchen and lifelong ministry to Detroit's poor via the Catholic Worker movement.

Lumpkin committed the remainder of his life (he is now in his eighties) to living and loving and serving the homeless.

"You never retire from your Christian vocation," he said. "You can always be a force for good [tov!]." Lumpkin said of his lifelong ministry to the homeless: "There are just a very few people who make this their life vocation. Most people that come stay for a few years and then move on."[17] Why did the Catholic Worker movement do what it did? Consider its mission:

> The Catholic Worker Movement . . . was an attempt to answer the question as old as Christianity: How can the Christian believer live justly in society?[18]

Person after person has learned from its living examples how to serve the poor in their communities. People notice—and follow—the life-giving example. Emulation leads to transformation.

DEEP TRANSFORMATION

The surest way for transformation agents and transformation coalitions (see chapter 6) to spur deep transformation in a church is first to become examples of the vision that the church wants to communicate. We can't say it often enough: *Emulation is the first principle of formation and transformation.*

Warm Up

1. What kind of example do you think you are to people in your church? Explain.

2. How would you describe your current lifestyle?

3. If you reproduced what you *do* (not what you teach), what would you be reproducing?

Get Some Insight

1. Ask five people who know you well to pick ten words they believe accurately describe your character. What insights do you gain from these words?

2. Carefully read Deuteronomy 6:1-9 and list ten things you learn about the importance of your own example.

3. In Philippians 4:9, Paul writes, "Whatever you have learned or received or heard from me, or seen in me—put it into practice." How would people in your church begin to act if you said the same thing to them about yourself that Paul said to the Philippians—and they did it? What kind of church would you have?

Do the Hard Work

1. If it's true that "transformation will happen only through emulation," what might need to change in your life?

2. Name several individuals in your sphere of influence who could join you as a band of Christians who begin to walk in the way of Jesus so well that others see Jesus in how that community of faith lives. What steps would you have to take to make that "band of Christians" a reality?

3. Which do you value most, the measurement of numerical enhancements in your church or the measurement of character formation in your church? Explain. How could you begin to measure character formation?

4. What ministries, organizations, or other churches in your area might be able to help, guide, or encourage you in your attempts to transform your church culture? If you don't know of any, do some research to locate a few such resources.

5. Hunt down at least three stories (currently unknown to you) that can instruct and encourage you in your efforts to transform the culture of your church.

PART 2

THREE PIVOTAL PRACTICES

6

BUILD A COALITION

THE MOST COMMON TEMPTATION for those less experienced with culture transformation is to think like this:

> We have a toxic culture.
> We need to transform our culture from toxic to tov.
> Let's replace it with a completely tov culture.
> *Sis, boom, bah!* Let's go!

So the preacher works up a cracking good sermon series on the word *good* in the Bible; the worship team finds songs that include the word *good* or writes some new songs about it; the youth leaders contextualize *good* for the youth culture; the Sunday school classes are all over the word *good*; the greeters have buttons with "Good! You are Here" in bright colors; and even the parking attendants have neon shirts with "Good Guy" in big bold letters. *Good* becomes the word.

We're assuming this has never happened, but you get the point.

This is most certainly *not* how to transform a culture. To use our image of a peach tree, all you have done is paint the tree.

The overall aim, of course, satisfies what the Bible teaches us: to be tov not only as individuals, but also as a group. But no one becomes totally tov, or Christlike, just because he or she wants to. Christlikeness, in other words, is a goal that's too big for a culture change. Instead, list specific items you want to change and then work on them, one at a time, one step at a time (see chapter 7).

Transforming a culture requires more than changing a few things that will do no more than adjust something in the old culture. Putting a woman on the platform will not make the weekday workplace less sexist. Culture transformation is not like hiring a tree removal service—yanking out the diseased peach tree and planting a new one in the old soil. You will learn, no doubt, that the disease was not in the tree but in the acids and chemicals and toxins still in the soil. You first need to degrade those toxins and then upgrade what is tov, so that tov nutrients can flow into the tree to produce tov fruit. One by one, one step at a time, you work on degrading the toxins in the soil by replacing them with tov nutrients. In time, your peach tree will start producing healthy fruit because the tree is now growing in healthy soil.

> You must redefine the "culture problem" at the outset—what is your goal in conducting a culture assessment? It makes no sense to engage in an involved assessment project to diagnose the culture without first having some definition of the presenting problem and what you might seek to change.
>
> EDGAR SCHEIN, *ORGANIZATIONAL CULTURE AND LEADERSHIP*

ONE HABIT TO BREAK

You can best frame the question in culture transformation by asking, "What is the *one habit* of our culture that we want to break and then transform?" or, "What is wrong that we want to transform?" Be specific. What do you want to transform, and why do you want to transform it?

Consider one good example. In her new book *Saving Grace*, political columnist and analyst Kirsten Powers vulnerably explains the discomfort in her own soul—how she had become angry, hostile, and even hateful toward those with whom she disagreed on political platform issues.[1] It's one thing for most of us to admit to ourselves, or even to our friends, that we find the other party disgusting. It's quite another for a national writer with strong opinions and a sharp pen to confess the same problems. Kirsten did. She explored her past with her therapist and came to terms with herself.

We might call her stories charming, but a better description would be that she came to terms with some ugliness for all of us to see. Her book is a redemptive read. When she wanted to change that one thing about herself, she landed on the Christian virtue of grace. So she worked on transformation, aiming to begin treating others with grace. She has told me (Scot) personally that her friends all comment on how much of a transformation they've seen in her.

A pastor friend of mine told me the one thing his church wanted to transform was no small thing: They wanted to shift from a simplistic "let's get born again" gospel to a Kingdom gospel. Instead of preaching a gospel that said little more than "Jesus loves you; you are a sinner; Jesus died for you; believe in him," the leaders of this church wanted to expand it to include the biblical conviction that believing requires lifelong discipleship training to live the way of Jesus in our world. That *way* includes caring about justice, compassion, and peace. For such a transformation to occur, many other dimensions of the church also needed to shift—adult Bible classes, relationships with one another, foreign missions trips, giving, and others. But the leaders wisely chose to focus on the single biggest issue they saw: their vision of the gospel. *That* was the one thing they wanted to transform. They grew convinced that their gospel had become too small and didn't match the Kingdom message of Jesus in the Gospels. Ultimately, their long-term planning, plotting, teaching, waiting, and praying worked—and now, some seven or eight years later, they have a transformed culture.

It *is* possible to transform a culture.

We recently read about a megachurch's senior pastor whose staff described him as *harsh*. He had earned a reputation for a top-down, dominance, and power-through-fear approach to running "his" church. They needed to transform this pervasive habit of abusive leadership.

This church now tells a different story, one of hope.

The church became willing to look honestly at the pastor. As a result, it hired a genuinely independent consulting firm to investigate the staff's claims. Rather than responding to the staff's concerns with denials, blame-shifts, gaslighting, and appeals to the pastor's authority, the church's leaders opened up conversations, listened to staff members, and asked hard questions that brought honest answers. The independent consulting group confirmed the staff's observations. The senior pastor was, in fact, harsh and authoritarian. Upon learning of these disturbing conclusions, "the church's Constitution Committee unanimously agreed to recommend that the board decline to restore [the pastor from his voluntary leave], prompting his resignation."[2]

The church focused on truth and tov, combining that with a commitment to honoring those people who had been mistreated by a spiritually abusive pastor. Leaders discerned, resisted, and now have begun to remove the toxic elements from the soil of their church's culture.

Laura and I have heard stories like this over and over in the past year. But abuse can work both ways; we also have heard stories of toxic churches who abuse their pastor and his family.

THE ONE QUESTION

The question "What one thing do we want to transform?" arises only because of something that many people perceive as unsatisfying, or not biblical enough, or inconsistent with a church's mission. In other words, they desire transformation only because of discovery. A desire for culture transformation happens only because someone (and

probably more than one person) clearly senses something wrong—
and that something is serious.

Mike Lueken of Oak Hills Church spotted something wrong that
pervaded both his own life and that of his church.

> I was disappointed with the wide gap between what I
> claimed to believe and who I actually was when I was off
> stage and behind closed doors. I was disappointed with my
> anger. I was disappointed by "mature" Christians who acted
> like spoiled children. I was disappointed with the dog-and-
> pony show of large church ministry.[3]

Other than sensing that something's not right, resulting in doing
a cultural study of your church, crises also can drive an organization's transformational urgency. Sometimes those crises reveal a dis-
connect between what the church is and what the church should be
or wants to be.

We don't mean that your church
needs a crisis to initiate culture
transformation. Crises can, however, become catalytic moments of
disconfirmation, conversation, and
discovery. They can reveal previously
hidden values and assumptions.

A desire for change, for doing something differently, for learning something new, always begins with some kind of pain or dissatisfaction.

EDGAR SCHEIN, *ORGANIZATIONAL CULTURE AND LEADERSHIP*

Pay close attention to how your
church or organization responds to a crisis, for its response "will
reveal deep elements of the culture."[4] We have seen crises provoke
toxic church responses, and we have seen beautifully breathtaking
(tov) responses to crises. Both reveal character and culture and active
agents at work beneath the surface.

WHAT'S THE "ONE THING" IN THIS STORY?

Over the last three years, we have received many letters of despair
from individuals who have experienced power and spiritual abuse at

the hands of a leader. We give but one example, distorting a detail or two to mask the identity of the institution.

A woman with gifts of leadership asked the lead pastor at her church a simple question: "When you have meetings where overall church strategy is discussed, is there ever a time you would invite me so I could participate?"

Seems like a good question from someone who cares.

The pastor gave a totally unacceptable response. Within two weeks, the woman was released from her leadership position, even though she had never received a single negative evaluation of her work. While it would be easy to get drawn into the swirling vortex of such a reprehensible act of power, we'll avoid that.

Here's our question: *What's the one thing wrong here that needs transformation?* Let's think aloud together.

Imagine that a deacon or elder board heard about the pastor's revenge and decided to investigate. The elders do a thorough search, some kind of culture survey, and discover that the pastor who sought revenge on this woman had done similar things many times before. Then they learn of the complicity of other leaders, that the human resources department refused to investigate complaints, and on and on, discovery after discovery. Suddenly the elders realize, *There's something wrong here.* And they know they must do something about it.

How do you change a culture like this? You can't change it by being a bully or by coercion or through verbal abuse. You may feel tempted to do a sermon series or a staff retreat that concentrates on tov culture—you know, to get the job done fast and then move forward.

But cultures don't get transformed like that. Oh, you can effect a superficial change easily enough: write up a policy and get everyone to sign a form promising never to verbally abuse anyone on staff. That's top-down. It might help some, but real, lasting, and deep transformation requires profound thinking, frequent discussions, real interactions, and getting everyone (or some kind of coalition) on board for culture transformation. It requires digging into the soil, not trimming branches. Top-down actions can change a particular item in an existing culture, but they never transform the culture itself.

This church elder board wanted to pivot; they wanted a transformation in which power was shared, people were treated as God's children made in God's image, existing staff received accurate and compassionate evaluations with measurable goals of growth, and other leaders who asked questions received fair hearings. That is, they wanted a church in which people with power treated others with honor and respect. They wanted to form a *people-first* culture.

How does a church accomplish this kind of deep transformation? Once you discern your church's culture and identify the one key area that most needs transformation, the next step is the most important yet. You must avoid top-down *powering over* the staff and congregation. You must pause and ponder how to *build a coalition* around the vision for transformation.

FOUR PHASES OF FORMING A COALITION-BASED PROPOSAL

What follows here is a suggested process that must be tailored to your specific institution:

> *Work slowly,*
> *With trusted colleagues,*
> *Toward the formation of a coalition*
> *And a proposal for transformation of your culture.*

Jumping in without clearly formed ideas will backfire. You want genuine ownership if you are serious about deep, lasting culture transformation. If you lack ownership, fractures will form that can split the church or ruin the possibility of transformation. One pastor told me that if he and his church had not worked for genuine ownership, they would have achieved nothing.

Hemant Kakkar and Niro Sivanathan studied top-down leadership characterized by dominance, competitiveness, and aggression.

They showed that such forms of leadership turn workers into individuals with a zero-sum mindset that minimizes helping one another and prevents teamwork and genuine ownership.[5] By contrast, we form coalitions, not top-down, but by organized listening.

We recommend thinking of leadership in the terms of political theorist Nannerl Keohane, who said that "leaders determine or clarify goals for a group of individuals and bring together the energies of members of that group to accomplish those goals."[6] Anne-Marie Slaughter, who led me to that definition by Keohane, describes leadership in terms of either a "vertical hierarchy of dominance," where the goal is to be on top, or as a "horizontal web of connection," where the goal is to be in the center. Center leaders form coalitions by listening and coalescing voices, while top leaders are didactic and demanding.[7]

Slaughter also learned that networking centers can function analogously to hierarchies of *power over*. How so? In a network, the margins are the least networked and thus have no voice. So, effectively working from the center also requires connection with those on the margins.[8] Thus, genuine coalitions can form only if the leader works from the center *and* from the margin. But Slaughter observed something else worthy of reflection: A coalition built from the center and from the margins is not a *consensus*, because a consensus approach almost always grants power to the most vocal and obnoxious.[9]

Churches that have transformed their culture, we have learned, did it by working on single problems and by following a four-layered process: (1) identifying one problem and pondering a solution; (2) developing ownership; (3) forming a transformation coalition; and (4) constructing a proposal for the congregation. At times, these four phases will be fluid, overlapping with other phases.

Do not gloss over the task of identifying the precise problem and dimension you want to transform. Take care not to misidentify it. You must carefully and accurately clarify the identified problem. As you go through the phases, you will almost always clarify your original analysis.

All along, the key leader, whom we call the Transformation Agent

(TA), along with the Transformation Coalition (TC), must remain in prayer, in study of Scripture, in reading intelligent studies about transformation, and in continual discernment of the Lord's will.

Phase 1: The TA Identifies One Problem and Ponders a Solution

The process of transformation usually begins, as all awakenings do, with a person in a position to do something about it suddenly realizing something has gone terribly wrong. A fair number of pastors have told us about their church transformations. The stories they tell tend to sound a lot like the story told by Kent Carlson and Mike Lueken, who as a twosome began to work on transforming Oak Hills.

We want to narrow the task a bit for a very simple reason. Like it or not, culture transformation at a church or an institution doesn't happen without an appointed person leading the transformation. Why not? Change and power are inextricably intertwined, as we discussed in chapter 4. Transformation often happens at the instigation of one key leader, whom we call the Transformation Agent (TA).

The TA in a church or Christian organization studies the Bible about the problem and ponders its solution. Let's call it the *theme*. The TA examines what the Bible says about the theme—for example, about tov. We recommend that the TA write down the most important elements of a theology of tov, with Bible verses attached (which will become handy before long). You can find an example of this (without the Bible references) in our book *A Church Called Tov*, through its listing of the Bible's key elements about goodness, or tov.

Here's what we learned:

1. God alone is tov and always does what is tov.
2. Everything God makes has a tov design.
3. Tov is something we *do*; it is active.
4. Tov counters evil: Those who do what is tov resist what is evil and run from it.
5. Tov expresses God's final and ultimate approval—those who are redeemed are declared by God to be tov.

6. The gospel itself, which is often translated as "Good News," is tov news or news about God's tov toward us.

7. Jesus is the man of tov.

These seven elements of tov gave us all kinds of insights into how we approached the problems of church abuses and toxicities. This is what we mean by articulating important elements of a biblical theme.

Each problem has its own articulation, shape, and contour, and every solution will mirror those contours and shapes. And almost every theme you can imagine has a shelf of books written about it. We encourage TAs not to shuffle down the row of books to the most recent study by some business leader about the topic (though, to be sure, those books often have profoundly useful action steps, as Edgar Schein's book *Organizational Culture and Leadership* did for us). Rather, we encourage TAs to dwell in the presence of the Lord while listening to the Word of God about a given topic. Dwelling in peaceful meditation on the Word often provokes the deepest insights and most significant action steps. After dwelling in the Word, we recommend reading a handful of the best books. If you don't know which books are the best, ask around of those who may know.

In the closing steps of phase 1, begin to make connections on paper between the problem, the solution you think could be best, the church's theology, and the church's mission statement. Also consider how the possible solution will work itself out practically (who does what and when and how). Ask how the proposed solution will affect the church socially and how it will affect other ministries in the church. At this point, you are only at a level somewhere between wondering and suggesting. Please don't lock down yet! Locking down may be the biggest temptation and the worst decision. Write down your best ideas on a half sheet of paper, or on a single page in your Moleskine notebook, and share them with some trusted colleagues to test and improve them.

Phase 2: The TA Develops Ownership

TAs can get the transformation process started only with the help of trusted associates in leadership. Without helpers, any thought of culture transformation will go up in smoke before it even gets off the ground. Schedule a meeting with your closest colleague. Go through what you see as the problem and ask for feedback. Listen well. Write down your colleague's thoughts and responses.

Let us say it again: *Listen well.* This is not about *you*; it's about a congregation of other people. Have you articulated the problem well? Does your closest associate agree? How might it be articulated better? Ask your colleague, "Am I wrong?" Listen to the response. And make sure he or she doesn't tell you only what you want to hear.

Next, share with your closest associate your biblical theology of a solution, and identify how the church has hopped the rails. Get into a conversation about it. Again, listen well. And then listen some more. Jot down ideas. Ask your associate whether the culture transformation you envision is worth the effort. If it is, ask for a commitment from that person to study through your Bible notes and then meet again to see if he or she has the same ideas, better ones, or complementary and supplementary suggestions. Build out a larger biblical theology of the theme. Finally, on the basis of this interaction, compose a better articulation of the problem and solution.

Now repeat the process with at least two other associates, perhaps as many as a group of four or five. Do everything all over again. Discern whether a coalition and a sense of unity are forming. If not, don't proceed until your trusted associates come close to agreement on the theme (the problem and its basic solution).

If the key leaders of a church or organization are not on board and on the same page, rebirth will likely not happen.

A PASTOR FRIEND

In all this, stay focused on only the most significant problem and its solution. It's spectacularly easy for the conversations to get bigger and broader until you feel ready to be elected president of the United States so you can solve global problems!

Your circle of colleagues has now formed into a small coalition. You are still only in the shallows, but you want to go deeper. All along, the TA and associates must remain in prayer and discernment of the Lord's will.

Phase 3: The TA Forms a Transformation Coalition

The time has come to expand your circle of friends into a coalition with wide ownership. Present to all your key leaders (including staff and others) your perceptions of the problem (e.g., too much power-mongering) and the solutions (e.g., practicing the tov life of loving others as yourself). Follow the same process as before: present the problem, remaining both vulnerable and open to correction and improvement. Listen to suggestions that can improve your articulation of the one problem and its solution.

Test the ideas, and let the ideas get bested by others who make suggestions. You are not only gaining a Transformation Coalition, but also acquiring ownership and buy-in from others. Listen, build, expand, and clarify your problem and its solution. Hide nothing. If you find resistance, listen especially well because the resistance you hear from this trusted circle will surely return later, only in a bigger and more powerful form. Don't dismiss suggestions that seem off the wall. And don't start firing people who aren't on board. You're not even *close* to transforming the culture of your church until you have listened to potential problems, considered carefully the resistance, and begun to formulate a reasonable and loving response to such resistance.

A Transformation Coalition is now forming; for some, it will remain in flux. Without this TC, any hope of culture transformation is doomed to failure. If you can't form such a coalition of leaders, don't make the change. You can still turn back.

REALITY CHECK BEFORE PHASE 4

In the best of all possible worlds, the TA will form a persuasive proposal for culture transformation, and everyone will immediately acclaim the idea as the best concept in the world.

But since we don't live in the best of all possible worlds, we need a reminder that even this early attempt to get key people on board for a culture transformation will encounter ditches, trips, falls, and fall-outs. It may involve a resistance bloc that sees your efforts as ridiculous, if not heretical. Or there may be some who believe the general idea isn't bad, but needs adjustments and changes.

Keep listening.

You can't transform a culture until you get a critical mass on board—or if not entirely on board, at least convinced to participate in the transformation. Ideally, they will be so convinced that they come to think of the whole thing as their own idea.

NEW HOPE: BUILDING A COALITION

Avoiding a top-down, coercive process lies at the core of a genuine transformation of church culture. A coalition must form, which is what happened at New Hope in Portland. John Rosensteel speaks of the beginnings of their coalition like this:

> In the midst of those dark days, God was faithful in many ways. God brought new staff, gifted men and women who felt called to help us build something new. A core of mature and committed people stayed and had the courage and grit to imagine and create a different type of church. Unexpectedly, other pastors and churches rallied to our side. I will be forever grateful for all of those people who came alongside us to bear the load.[10]

Like Oak Hills, New Hope rethought its handling of the gospel itself, not because they rethought the New Testament, but because they came to believe they had adopted a "shrunken gospel." As John Rosensteel put it,

> The shrunken gospel is enough to *save* us, but not enough to *change* us. It doesn't place a call upon our lives to become disciples. It promises life after death instead of life now. Our

church has begun to embrace the full gospel. Jesus died and rose again to make us right with God, with one another, and with the world. We don't have to wait to live. We can start experiencing eternal life right now.[11]

Their coalition formed around a vision, expressed in words that may be some of the most important for other churches to hear: "As it became clearer who God was calling us to become, we were freed from being the church we no longer were."[12] Measuring attendance ceased to matter at New Hope. In fact, John told us, "If there is a market for a book about how to downsize a church, we could write it."[13] Oak Hills could be the coauthor.

Phase 4: The TA Constructs a Proposal for the Congregation

Once you've formed a Transformation Coalition, regather with your closest associates to put the final touches on identifying the one problem and articulating your best solution for it. Process together all the feedback you have received. Build your big ideas into a proposal and put it all on one piece of paper. Don't hurry to form the proposal.

> Be aware that some of your early champions, including the people who hired you, will leave. This often happens. They hired you to bring change, but once change comes, they don't always like it. Though it's a hard thing to stomach, it almost always becomes a reality.
>
> A PASTOR FRIEND

A pastor friend told me (Scot) that he went through all four Gospels, line by line, reflecting on a given theme with his entire team. They met every other week and the process took a complete year. By the time they finished, lights had gone on for many and a TC formed spontaneously. Only then had the time come to move to the congregation, to present to the people the beginnings of a culture transformation. (When my friend and I met for breakfast recently, the process was working well.)

All along, the TA and the TC must remain in prayer to discern the Lord's will. No matter the theme—love, tov, justice, servant leadership, spiritual formation—the most potent dimension for many in the congregation will be a living, breathing, and trustworthy example.

We like to talk about Mr. Rogers (as you've seen in this book), and I (Scot) like to appeal to Dietrich Bonhoeffer. Both provide good examples, but the single most important element of education is not *information*, but *emulation* of someone with whom one has a relationship. The ideal is for the TA, along with the principal members of the TC, to be living examples of the theme of transformation.

To church leaders, we say: Don't ask people to do what you yourselves are not doing. What you *do* will provide the most persuasive component of leading your church into transformation. (But that doesn't mean everyone will tag along.)

WILLING TO PAY THE PRICE?

A suburban congregation had experienced a few years of minor attendance decline, mostly attributed to longtime saints passing away and a few young families relocating for professional opportunities. The decline scared some of the church leaders enough that they reached out to a growing multisite church to learn about the possibility of a congregational merger.

The conversation progressed to the point that the church took a formal vote, but a narrow majority decided not to merge with the expanding city congregation. However, the congregation was now clearly divided. It was at this point that a pastor friend was hired.

Everyone wanted *some* level of change, but there was no consensus on what to do. As the new pastor listened to his congregation, he heard the pain and the fear deep inside each individual and within the entire culture. As the primary Transformation Agent, he discerned that empathy and putting people first needed the most focus. He attempted to create a Transformation Coalition with the established leadership, but they wanted no part of mending damaged relationships. Many instead chose to leave. Within eight months of the pastor's arrival, the entire search committee that had called him to the church also left.

Fortunately, the story didn't end there. Over the course of several years, the church found level ground and began creating new ministries to serve the congregation and its neighborhood.

Remember this: *All culture transformation involves fallout,* and the TA and TC members must discern whether they are willing to pay the price for that fallout.

Warm Up

1. What's wrong with trying to move too fast when attempting to transform the culture of an unhealthy church or organization?

2. Name some examples of trying to transform a culture merely by adjusting a thing or two in the old, unhealthy culture. What happened as a result?

3. Describe some "painting the tree" exercises you have seen churches try in their attempts at culture transformation.

Get Some Insight

1. What is the one habit of your culture that you want to break and then transform? Talk over this question with one or two trusted associates.

2. Ask, "What is wrong in our culture that we want to transform?" Be specific.

3. *Why* do you want to transform this element? Be specific.

4. What kind of pain or dissatisfaction is driving your desire for culture transformation?

5. How does your church or organization tend to respond to crises? What does this response reveal to you?

Do the Hard Work

1. In phase 1 of culture transformation, the Transformation Agent identifies one problem and ponders a solution.

   a. Who in your church or organization is in a position to do something about the "one problem" identified?

b. Have the TA study the Bible about the identified cultural problem and ponder possible solutions to it. The TA then identifies the theme.

c. Write down the most important theological elements of this theme, attaching the relevant biblical references to it.

d. Dwell in the presence of the Lord while listening to God's Word about this theme.

e. Read a handful of good books on the theme.

f. Begin to make connections on paper between the problem, a possible solution, the church's theology and mission statements, and how the proposed solution might work itself out practically (who does what, when, and how?).

g. How will this proposed solution affect the church or organization socially? How will it affect other church ministries or organizational departments?

h. Do *not* lock down yet on the solution or your inquiry!

i. On a half sheet of paper, write down your best ideas and discuss them with trusted colleagues, with the goal of improving them.

2. In phase 2, the TA develops ownership.

a. Schedule a meeting with your closest colleague. Rehearse what you see as the problem and ask for feedback. Write down the colleague's thoughts and responses. Ask, "Am I wrong here?"

b. Share with your closest associate your biblical theology of a solution and how your church or organization has hopped the rails. Have a conversation about it. Jot down ideas.

c. Ask your associate whether the culture transformation you envision is worth the effort. If so, ask for a commitment from your associate to study through your Bible notes and then meet again to see whether her or she has the same ideas (or better ones, complementary ones, or supplementary suggestions).

d. Build out a larger biblical theology of the theme.

e. On the basis of this interaction, compose a better articulation of the problem and your proposed solution.

f. Do the same thing with at least two others (perhaps as many as a

group of four or five). Discern whether a unified coalition is forming. If not, don't proceed until your trusted associates come close to
agreement on the theme (i.e., the problem and its solution).

g. Stay focused on only the most significant problem and its solution.

h. Remain in prayer, trying to discern the Lord's will.

3. In phase 3, the TA forms a Transformation Coalition (TC).

a. Expand your circle of friends into a coalition with wide ownership.
Present to all key leaders your perceptions of the problem and the
solutions. Remain open to correction and improvement. Listen to
suggestions that can improve your articulation of the one problem
and its solution.

b. Test the ideas you get; allow them to be bested by others who make
suggestions. Listen, build, expand, and clarify your problem and its
solution. Hide nothing.

c. If resistance surfaces, listen especially well, because the resistance
you hear from this trusted circle will surely return later, only in a bigger and more powerful form. Don't dismiss suggestions that seem
off the wall. Don't start firing people who aren't on board.

d. Remember, you are not even *close* to transforming your culture
until you have listened to potential problems, considered carefully
the resistance, and started to formulate a reasonable and loving
response to the resistance.

e. If you can't form a coalition of leaders, don't make the change. You
can still turn back.

4. In phase 4, the TA constructs a proposal for the congregation.

a. Regather with your closest associates to put final touches on identifying the one problem and articulating your best solution for it.
Process together all the feedback you have received.

b. Build your big ideas into a proposal and put it all on one piece of
paper. Don't hurry to form the proposal.

c. Remain in prayer to discern the Lord's will.

d. The most potent dimension for many in the congregation will be a living, breathing, and trustworthy example. Remember, the single most important element of education is not *information* but *emulation* of someone with whom one has a relationship. The TA, along with the principal members of the TC, must be the living examples of the chosen theme of transformation.

e. Never ask people to do what you yourself are not doing.

7

TAKE ONE STEP
AT A TIME

DO YOU KNOW WHAT IT'S LIKE to get a group of professors, many of them beyond (or well beyond) the sixty-year-old milestone, to change what they are doing? I (Scot) do.

When I taught at North Park University, our dean, who by the nomenclature in this book was a Transformation Agent working like the dickens to form a Transformation Coalition, decided we needed to implement an Outcome-Based Education (OBE) model. The dean and associates explained things and walked through the next couple of years, one step at a time.

First step: The selling point of this model, deeper than a deep-culture transformation, was that it was learner-centered and not teacher-centered. (Don't forget, we're talking here about professors.) Besides the obviously exaggerated branding and alienating language that calls most instruction teacher-centered, the big idea was that we assess learning and growing *in skills* more than through the objective measure of a test or exam.

Second step: The dean decided to work with a couple of TA-appointed professors who formed an early coalition with the dean.

Third step: One of the selling points was that we would go through a school-wide accreditation process—there were plenty of groans already just in hearing the word *accreditation*—in some three or four years, to which Professor So-and-So already had been appointed. We all valued this professor so highly that we at least shifted a little to the approval side of OBE.

> I heard once that a dean's job description is like running a zoo with all the cages open.

Several more steps followed. The process of forming a coalition began with several departments gathering into faculty groups. There we learned the theory behind OBE. The professor who was presenting did a decent job of explaining it, but the meeting broke down somewhat when people began to ask questions. Only later did I learn why. We needed some really good examples, not bare theory. Since no one in the room had ever done OBE, everything was based on a theory that no one believed in or had ever attempted.

Not long afterward came my turn to take a few steps.

As the chair of the biblical and theological studies (BTS) department, I did not feel at all convinced that OBE was the way to go. But I listened and tried to figure things out because it was my responsibility to get our department approved by the accreditation team. Even more, *we had no choice.* The dean had committed to an OBE approach for assessment to prepare us for accreditation, and Professor So-and-So had the full-time task of pulling together the various department assessments into a school-wide (and probably thousand-page) report to the accreditation institution (whose name I have blocked from my memory).

Thinking it was my task to implement OBE in my department, I ordered a couple of books, did some reading and some more research, learned about Alverno College in Milwaukee where OBE is next to God, and attended a two-day conference designed to teach unsuspecting and unwilling old professors what OBE was and how it worked.

Suddenly it clicked for me, and I became an evangelist for OBE in our department.

I tried to clarify things for the others, one step at a time. Because a class syllabus matters immensely, I concentrated on how to write an OBE-shaped syllabus. I wrote pages of instructions with illustrations on how to adjust the syllabus and classroom lectures into a more learner-centered approach.

First step: Articulate at the top of the syllabus the major outcomes for each class we would teach. Outcomes are measurable actions a student *will be able to do* (note that phrase) as a result of the class. As in, "The student will be able to define what Jesus meant by 'Kingdom of God.'" I numbered each outcome for our courses and asked the professors to adjust the outcomes they thought vital for their courses.

One step at a time.

Textbooks didn't change. The real kick in the shins was combining *every* assignment in the syllabus with one of the numbered outcomes. Each outcome also connected to the overall outcomes of our department, which we discussed and came to a "consensus" about.

Amazingly, our one-step-at-a-time approach worked. We got approved, eventually.

I tell this story not as an example of a successful transformation of a department or a culture, but as an illustration of learning about OBE, how it worked, and how we implemented it in each class session so that the focus became more learner-centered than teacher-centered. To this day, I cannot write a syllabus without thinking about the coherence between outcomes and a specific day in class. For me, it was a key lesson in the essence of culture transformation: *Take one step at a time.*

STEPS IN THE JOURNEY TOWARD TOV

We assume you know your ultimate goal and that you have several ways to express that goal. Oak Hills talked about spiritual transformation, while another church spoke of a Kingdom-shaped church. In our projects together, Laura and I work toward the goal of a tov culture, which includes at least the seven elements in the Circle of Tov:

- empathy
- grace
- putting people first
- telling the truth
- justice
- service
- Christlikeness

You could use sections of the Bible that speak to the formation of character, some of which we've already outlined:

- the Ten Commandments
- the major moral themes of the prophets
- the instructions of Jesus in the Sermon on the Mount
- the fruit of the Spirit
- any other major ethical category in the Bible (godliness, faithfulness, love, etc.)

Enumerate your master list that expresses genuine Christian character and begin the journey toward tov, or toward greater Christlikeness, in yourself and in your congregation.

Again, one step at a time. We hope the nine suggestions that follow may prove helpful.

1. Ordering

Identify the character challenges your church faces and *rank them in order of importance* for your church. Once you have formed your Transformation Coalition and the proposal has been enacted in your church, start moving toward tov by working on one theme per year, beginning with the highest priority.

Oak Hills formed "One Thing" groups where the goal was to "pursue spiritual formation in one specific area." That is, "Each person spent a month or so attending to their one thing" and learned that the one thing led to seeing deeper issues that needed attention.[1]

We suggest you set out a plan, ranked from most important to least important, of the "one thing" issues you want to work on.

2. Emulating

As mentioned in the previous chapter, we learn more through emulation than information. Thus, a vital, if not crucial, step in transforming your church culture is to find good examples of tov. In other words, raise up examples that mirror your proposal.

We need sterling examples of tov that others can witness, confirmed by all who know the individuals in their home lives, their work lives, and their public lives. Though we should not deify any human, we can all find good examples of a tov life to emulate.

I (Scot) have lived long enough to see some examples of individuals who I thought were wonderfully tov people, only to learn later that they weren't. When Laura and I wrote *A Church Called Tov*, she often sent me examples of current churches and pastors for us to consider including in the book. I usually vetoed them and said, "Wait till they're dead. Then we'll know for sure." That is one reason we highlighted the life of Fred Rogers. His tov-ness proved true to the end. But in your local context, where you know people personally and can observe them over time, you will want to look for living, breathing, examples of tov to emulate.

3. Teaching

A third step is to clearly, carefully, and comprehensively *teach* the proposal for your church culture transformation. Your experience of the Transformation Agent and his or her close associates studying the Bible and reading good literature on some identified culture transformation becomes your grid for teaching. Anchor your teaching in clear biblical passages and break it down into digestible and memorable elements, one day at a time, one week to the next. One six-week series will never do it. A congregation can absorb culture transformation only if the main ideas are taught repeatedly and given the power to penetrate *everything*.

REALITY CHECK BEFORE MOVING ON

The heart of this chapter is about patience, time, and culture trans-formation. How long did it take to form the current culture in your church? We're guessing it took as many as twenty years, maybe fifty. It takes a long time for a way of life to become a fixed culture.

If you want tov to form in your own culture, you must make a commitment to a long-term, slow, step-by-step process of knocking out toxicity and pursuing goodness. We love how Kent Carlson said this (notice the realism in his words): "When we unplugged from the high-octane, entrepreneurial, pragmatic, success-driven, attractional model of church growth, our church was plunged into a decade-long roller-coaster ride of excessive (at times) introspection, organiza-tional upheaval, uncertainty, plummeting attendance, and fractured relationships. . . . It has been a costly journey."[2]

Have you heard the witty illustration of how one can move the church piano from one side of the platform to the other without upsetting the congregation? One inch a week. If you slide it from one side to the other on a Thursday afternoon, you are likely to hear about it before you get home from Sunday services. But if you move it one inch a week, you will likely never hear about it because no one will notice.

Less witty and more real, a pastor friend said to me (Scot), "Patience is imperative. Most cultural rebirths take seven years. If you cut corners and try to rush it, you will pay. The primary reason for this is that most healthy people leave an unhealthy culture early. When rebirthing, you usually start with a group of pretty unhealthy people. It takes time for the right people to arrive."

The one-step-at-a-time approach anticipates that it takes years, not weeks or months, to transform a culture. The deeper the toxicity, the longer it takes to transform it into tov.

Leaders deeply involved in organizational transformation agree with my pastor friend quoted above. It takes *seven years* to transform a culture. So let's agree that's an acceptable ballpark figure. One step at a time, indeed!

Some on your TC will move away, new people will move in, some will die, some will marry, some will divorce, some will step back, and some will step forward.

One step at a time.

Stay in it for the long haul. Several good words appropriate for this reality might include *grit*, *perseverance*, *persistence*, *composure*, *faithfulness*, and *daily*.

4. Doing

Changing an athletic habit requires twenty-seven hours of doing the new behavior correctly, or so we are told. You can't change your ability to lift a golf ball out of the sand and make it spin and stop on a green by reading about it in a Ben Hogan book. You must step into a sand trap with your sand wedge, get baskets of golf balls, and swing, swing, swing. Along with a good instructor guiding you to do it correctly.

In a similar way, learning a new language requires repeated, intentional practice. For the first time in my twenty years in public education, I (Laura) am teaching a 100 percent non-English-speaking student. She is immersed in the English language with her new teachers and classmates and is learning and absorbing by listening, watching, and doing.

One word at a time.

The most important act of transforming your church culture is to establish new behaviors that can form into a culture deep enough to influence others to mimic the behavior. Becoming a putting-people-first congregation requires actions repeated often enough to become instinctive, as we saw with the hospitality of the people of Gander, Newfoundland, and the refugee-welcoming residents of Le Chambon, France. When a group of your people habituates into a putting-people-first culture, you will see congregational transformation. Those swimming in a people-first culture will be the first to recognize when the church gets out of line.

From beginning to end in this one-step-at-a-time approach, *doing* is the heart of culture transformation. Only in *doing* tov do people learn to *be* tov, and only in *being* tov does a culture form that *is* tov.

5. Illustrating

Find fresh illustrations of your proposal's big ideas. For culture transformation aligned with the Circle of Tov, we would find fresh examples of

- empathy
- grace
- putting people first
- telling the truth
- justice
- service
- Christlikeness

At the same time, learn to both recognize and walk away from narcissism, power-through-fear, institution creep, false narratives, misplaced loyalty, celebrity, and leadership obsessions. Other themes might also appear for church-shaping transformation, such as spiritual formation or God's Kingdom.

Find stories in church history—of women and persons of color, of people from other denominations. Shower your affirmations in all directions.

6. Exhorting and Encouraging

As a Transformation Agent, you and your Transformation Coalition will need to give routine *exhortation* and *encouragement*. If all of this could happen in one weekend retreat, we could skip to "Well done!" and get ready for a front-row seat to the "Glory Hallelujah" of heaven's choir! But don't pick your seat quite yet. This will take a long time. Discouragement will come, depression will set in, bewilderment will surround you, and most everyone will start wondering if it's worth it.

It is.

NEW HOPE: TRANSFORMATION'S ROUGH BEGINNINGS

At New Hope Church in Portland, John Rosensteel learned early that his new church had problems within problems, each with its own history. "We quickly learned that unhealthy cultures are typically far unhealthier than they initially appear to be."

To make budget, New Hope had to lay off one-fourth of its staff. One pastor got fired for inappropriate behavior. Another pastor started a new church within shouting distance of New Hope, which led some staff members to resign from New Hope to work at the new church.

"We were one month in and already it was a five-alarm dumpster fire," John said. New Hope soon picked up an unenviable nickname: *No Hope*. John knew he was called to pastor these people, but he also had no idea what to do to transform No Hope back into New Hope.

He admitted to us that those first couple of years were the worst of his entire pastoral ministry. Those who have experienced the kind of flourishing that John enjoyed with his previous congregation, Blackhawk Church in Madison, Wisconsin, often feel their failures the deepest. He got lost in the challenges, his marriage began to falter, friendships soured, and he came close to a massive heart attack. "On almost every level, I felt like a colossal failure," he said.[3]

To counteract and overcome the power of pessimism and despair, both the TA and the TC must become agents of encouragement and exhortation.

7. Mentoring

Preachers, teachers, and pastors trained in seminaries all tend to think that everything important happens in the Sunday morning service, and especially in their dearly beloved sermons. Not to put too fine a point on it, but we need to say it: Most people forget the sermon by 1 p.m. on Sunday.

For transformation to take place, we must deepen all preaching by *mentoring*. Pastors must mentor associates and staff, senior staff must mentor junior staff, youth pastors must mentor teens, etc. Moms and dads and singles and widows and widowers and other members all must be mentored and come to see themselves as mentors. Too many people equate pastoring with *preaching*, and the only things the congregants know about their pastor are from his sermons. That is not pastoring.

Genuine pastoring means mentoring, discipling, and working one-on-one. A pastor actually *shepherds* people. Pastors and other spiritual leaders spend time mentoring others in the seven habits in the Circle of Tov. One step at a time, one day at a time, one week at a time, over the long haul. (And we must do this in ways tailored to the recipients, at the pace they want, not the pace we may want.)

8. Interacting and Assessing

Have you caught the main idea? Culture transformation requires a commitment to making changes over time, one step at a time. It also involves both *interacting* and *assessing*.

Enthusiasts for big-ticket, quick proposals for transformation can get overcommitted to specific shifts and changes. But transformation doesn't work like that. Adjustments will have to be made even after you enter the promised land. To do this, the TA and the TC must interact with individuals in the congregation to see how they are progressing in tov transformation. They will also need to interact with groups within the church, such as the finance team or the outreach team or the director of young adult ministries. To return to this chapter's opening illustration, Outcome-Based Education emphasizes ongoing *assessment* in order to make adjustments tailored to real-life realities. That's true of culture transformation as well.

Suppose you are working on getting your congregation to do more works of service. Suddenly, you realize that while the young adults, the middle-aged, and the senior citizens are picking fruit from the tree in bushel baskets, the thirtysomethings are (to put it mildly) unengaged and relaxing in the shade of the tree. You also realize that a weekly or even monthly service assignment is not feasible for young parents with toddlers. You learn this by interacting with them and assessing that the service habits for folks in your church need to be adjusted according to the seasons of life. Seems simple, doesn't it? But you need to make it explicit that your church's situation requires constant interaction and ongoing assessment.

John Rosensteel learned culture transformation on the job.

One of the crucial lessons we learned was that churches, even healthy churches, often measure the wrong things. What we measure matters; it indicates a missional priority. Churches often measure attendance, giving, online clicks, and raised hands to indicate a decision for Jesus. These things are not unimportant but can be very misleading. They can give an indication of health when health does not exist. We are presently developing a tool that is in process to help our staff focus on the right things. We will likely have six questions for them to ask and answer before and after important events or as a consistent evaluative tool. We are hoping these questions enter the water of our culture and transform and clarify what we feel is most important.[4]

John developed a series of questions that New Hope's leaders ask about all substantive decisions. These questions emerged out of a *six-year* process of church culture transformation. Each of the six questions elicits an answer that helps to assess ongoing transformation in the church.

- Was this event/endeavor saturated in prayer?
- Was wisdom sought in the planning process?
- Was there opportunity for participation and practice?
- Were volunteers equipped and developed?
- Did we bring people together in a world that is coming apart?
- Did we walk in the way of the dragon or the way of the Lamb?[5]

Every flourishing ministry or organization routinely assesses itself and responds to clear indicators of things gone wrong. We never reach paradise when it comes to character formation for an entire congregation. We are always striving . . . until Kingdom come.

9. Reminding

Teaching is a key element in a one-step-at-a-time approach to culture transformation. Effective, ongoing teaching means *reminding* congregants of what you are doing, where you have been, what you have learned, and where you are headed. It's too easy to move on to the next big thing.

A church culture transformation locks down on the unchanging virtues of character—and we all need constant reminders. The word *remember* occurs 161 times in the New International Version, from God's saying, "I will remember my covenant" (Genesis 9:15) to the church in Sardis being told, "Remember, therefore, what you have received" (Revelation 3:3). Over and over, what *had been taught* was to be remembered.

Look up Deuteronomy 4:10; 5:15; 8:2; Joshua 1:13; Ecclesiastes 12:1; Isaiah 46:9; and Malachi 4:4. In the New Testament, look up John 15:20; 16:4; 2 Corinthians 9:6; and 2 Timothy 2:8. *Remembering* characterizes the continual education of God's people. A handful of attentive listeners may remember something taught just once; but teaching something over and over works its way into the minds and hearts and bones—and memory—and eventually forms a permanent part of a culture.

Warm Up

1. Why does creating a tov culture depend on taking one step at a time?

2. Have you ever been a part of something that rushed change? How did that go?

3. Which of the seven elements in the Circle of Tov (empathy, grace, putting people first, telling the truth, justice, service, Christlikeness) are least represented in your church or organization? Explain.

Get Some Insight

1. For you and your church or organization, what expresses genuine Christian character? Create a master list.

2. Describe the first step you need to take in your journey to a transformed church or organizational culture.

Do the Hard Work

We give nine steps of suggestions for effectively moving your church or organization toward a more tov culture.

1. *Ordering*: Identify the character challenges your church faces. Then rank them in order as seems best for your church. Set out a plan, ranked from most important to least important, of the "one thing" issues you want to work on.

2. *Emulating*: Identify good examples of tov in your church or organization. Why did you select these individuals?
   How can you raise up examples that mirror your proposal for change and transformation?

3. *Teaching*: Clearly, carefully, and comprehensively teach the proposal for your church or organizational culture transformation.

   Anchor your teaching in clear biblical passages and break it into digestible and memorable elements.

4. *Doing*: Remember that *doing* is the heart of culture transformation. Only in *doing* tov do people learn to *be* tov, and only in *being* tov does a culture form that *is* tov.

   What new behaviors do you need to establish in your church or organization that can help form a culture deep enough to influence others to emulate the same behavior?

5. *Illustrating*: Find fresh illustrations of your proposal's big ideas in church history, of women and persons of color, of people from other denominations. Use these illustrations to shower affirmation in all directions.

   At the same time, learn to both recognize and reject narcissism, power-through-fear, institution creep, false narratives, misplaced loyalty, celebrity, and leadership obsessions.

6. *Exhorting and Encouraging*: Make it a habit to routinely give exhortation and encouragement.

7. *Mentoring*: Deepen all preaching and teaching by mentoring. Let pastors mentor associates and staff, senior staff mentor junior staff, and youth pastors mentor youth.

   Find a way to mentor moms, dads, singles, widows, widowers, and all other members of the church or organization. Encourage them all to become mentors too.

8. *Interacting and Assessing*: Use or adapt these six questions developed by New Hope Church:

   a. Was this event/endeavor saturated in prayer?
   b. Was wisdom sought in the planning process?

c. Were there opportunities for participation and practice?

d. Were volunteers equipped and developed?

e. Did we bring people together in a world that is coming apart?

f. Did we walk in the way of the dragon or the way of the Lamb?

9. *Reminding*: Continually remind your people of what you are doing in the transformation process, where you have been, what you have learned, and where you are headed.

Read carefully and discuss with your associates several Bible passages, including: Deuteronomy 4:10; 5:15; 8:2; Joshua 1:13; Ecclesiastes 12:1; Isaiah 46:9; Malachi 4:4; John 15:20; 16:4; 2 Corinthians 9:6; and 2 Timothy 2:8. What do you learn about the importance of remembering from these passages? How will you incorporate what you learned into the culture of your church or organization?

8

CREATE POCKETS
OF TOV

THE FIRST WEEK AFTER *A Church Called Tov* became available, we
began to hear this response: "I'm in a toxic church culture. What can I
do to change the toxic culture to tov?" That quickly became the most
common question asked of us.

One example: A director of a ministry with people under him
and over him at a church in the South wrote to us a long account.
He noticed the direction of the church, heard concerns expressed
by fellow staffers about the church's tone and direction, and felt an
obligation to approach those above him about those concerns. When
the director saw the pastor walking into church one weekday morning, he approached him and asked a simple question: "When you
discuss strategy, is there any chance the ministry directors could be
involved?"

The pastor did not respond well, and the situation quickly went
downhill. In both manner and teaching, the pastor often echoed his
role model, a well-known megachurch leader notorious for a top-
down, authoritarian style. Consequently, the church's circle of power

was *not* the Circle of Tov. Many associates and directors were forced to do the bidding of the few who called the shots. This director, though at times publicly affirmed as a leader, had no more power than a regular attender. One month later, he found himself unemployed.

So again, here's the question we are repeatedly asked: *What can we do to transform a toxic culture?*

ONLY A FEW OPTIONS

We begin with a realistic reminder: Culture transformation occurs only if people with power use it for transformation toward tov.

And what about the powerless? After a speaking event at a church, a group of women approached me (Laura) with concerns about toxicities there. As women, they said, they were powerless because they are not permitted to be elders or pastors. What could they do in their situation?

Our responses have varied in the last year, but we know of only a few options. We offer here our best answers for those not in power or who feel powerless.

A SCENARIO REVISITED

Let's adjust a scenario we used in chapter 1, to give it a sharper edge. Suppose you are a female staff member at your church; you know people's names, and the pastor knows your name. In your presence he often says he likes having women on staff and that he's proud of the presence of women around the church. It gives the church a good reputation.

One day you notice the pastor in an office near you. You hear raised voices and wonder what's going on. Soon the pastor shuts the door—rather, he slams it—and storms off. It turns out it was the office of one of your closest female friends on campus.

A month later you witness something similar, with a male associate this time, but this time you overhear the conversation, including some harsh comments about another woman. Some of it sounds both ugly and sexist. You decide to tell a trusted friend on staff, and she responds that she's seen the same behavior over at least the past five years.

How can a pastor act like that? you wonder. You can't figure it out: How could people in the church permit such behavior, even though many have witnessed such outbursts?

Further conversations confirm that the pastor is indeed sexist, that he speaks in a derogatory fashion about women. He likes to have women on staff, but he makes sure they have no power at the table when decisions are made. He will tear down any woman who begins to gain respect and a following. You decide that this male toxicity has to stop, and you want to be part of the shifting toward a culture that respects women.

We have heard so many stories like this that we could write a book, but this is not that kind of book. We want to find a way to get everyone on a pathway toward tov. But how best to do that?

In some churches, this will mean forming pockets of tov that resist, quietly but effectively, the toxic powers and their expressions of the flesh.

SIX ASSUMPTIONS

Let's begin with six clear assumptions:

1. You are not in power, nor even close to having power.
2. You have seen and become concerned about toxic powers at work.
3. You have made an accurate assessment.
4. You want to do something about shifting your church culture toward tov.
5. You have spoken with someone in power and met strong pushback.

Pause.

6. You need to remind yourself that no church is perfect.

Let's be frank. Not everything that someone sees and thinks is toxic is indeed toxic. But in this chapter, we will assume that someone without access to power witnesses real toxicity in how the senior leaders treat women, and that such treatment has become systemic. Also, this person (you) wants to do something about it, but the powers that be don't seem to see the same toxicity that you see.

Over the last year or more, this has become the most common question asked of us: Why do I see it but they don't?

Each person must discern what to do. When I (Scot) discussed this issue with another pastor friend, he replied, "Tell them that if they are not in power or close to people in power, to leave. It will be much better for them." He wasn't being harsh. He was speaking very pastorally into realities he has witnessed both in his church and in churches among his circle of pastor friends.

A "WISHFUL IMAGE OF PIOUS COMMUNITY"

Let's clarify what we mean by "no church is perfect." Some church folks have what Dietrich Bonhoeffer called a "wishful image of pious community."[1] Many have unrealistic expectations of leaders, of other Christians, and of what the church is.

Churches are hospitals for sinners more than they are all-inclusive beach resorts for saints. We do not understand the church until we grapple with the truth that *we* are sinners, among other sinners, each one standing in line for the graces of the Lord's Supper. We need to forget and abandon our dreams of perfection.

At a church where I (Scot) spoke, the pastor took my wife, Kris, and me around to see the place. At one point she said, "It's not perfect. We are a messy bunch."

I muttered to myself, *That's what a church is. A mess of sinners bundled together.*

Mike Lueken calls a church "the fellowship of the unformed." He adds a flourish to this with a comment: "The people of God are a community of unrefined, unfinished, conflict-loving, trouble-causing, sin-committing, cranky hypocrites."[2] He's so right.

When we impose our idealistic, perfectionistic, high-expectation images of the church onto our actual churches, we begin to destroy them. As Dietrich Bonhoeffer said, "Those who love their dream of a Christian community more than the Christian community itself become destroyers of that Christian community, even though their personal intentions may be ever so honest, earnest, and sacrificial."[3]

So, what does this mean for anyone who wants to form a pocket of tov in their church? They need to ask if what they want to change is anything more than a messed-up feature of human sinners in fellowship with one another in Christ.

For the rest of this chapter, we will assume the issue *is* more than messy sinners, and that you want to move forward toward tov. Christian counselor Diane Langberg has often said that we must be healthy in a psychological sense to be able to confront toxic leadership with their toxicities. So get ready.

FORM A POCKET OF TOV

We advise those who want to stay at the table to form a "pocket of tov" in the middle of the toxic church culture. A pocket of tov requires us to commit to living as tov as possible, which means we attempt to do from the inside, without power, what tov agents in other contexts want to do for the whole church. And that means we strive to put into action the varied priorities, practices, and powers discussed in this book.

"But I have no power! And those *in* power don't like what they think I may be up to." This means you are a dissident forming a pocket of tov that over time may spawn enough other pockets of tov to create a critical mass of tov that can speak up with some strength about the toxicities. And make no mistake about it: Your pocket of tov is a pocket of resistance.

In his book *Biblical Ethics and Social Change*, Stephen Charles Mott discusses the periodic necessity for citizens to participate in "strategic noncooperation," which refers to "selective, socially potent forms of nonconformity."[4] Such tactics involve a form of respect for order. If enough people refuse to participate in some expected social norm, the institution observes resistance and perceives it as a serious threat to order. Nevertheless, in some cases, change leading to transformation may occur.

But in your case, how to move forward? If we can assume you are correct about your church's toxicities and that you want to move the church toward tov, you must begin by spending plenty of time in prayer, Bible study, and thinking about the one thing you believe needs to change. You may be correct that "the whole church is a filthy mess," but the only way forward is one step at a time.

You will need, as already discussed, to articulate what the Bible says about what is wrong in your church and about what should replace it. You will then need to find another person whom you can trust to discuss the situation by listening to one another carefully. This, too, takes time—more than one or two conversations, more than a week or two. Over time, branch out to a few others so you can form a pocket of tov. Begin to live out the tov-ness that needs to replace the toxicity. Pivot.

We've already gone too far without saying this, so we need to say it now: Most pastors will probably see you as schismatic and divisive. But *if* you are right about the toxicity in the church, and *if* you have no power, and *if* no one is willing to give you an ear—and *if you are committed to staying in this church and seeing this process through*—then creating a pocket of tov is your only way forward.

What toxic power agents see as schismatic might, in fact, be a revival in the making. You never know. But I do know this: *If* you are right about the toxicity, *it is worth it* to try to change it. Venezuela and Cuba resolve pockets of resistance through exile. Toxic powers prefer exile. Put kindly, people leave or get pushed out and gaslit. But millions of dissidents still live in Venezuela and in Cuba. Sticking it out, no matter the cost, is the only way to turn toxic into tov. Think Nelson Mandela and Desmond Tutu. Think of the underground Chinese churches.

You move toward goodness with others in a pocket of tov. You live with an obligation to tov that conflicts with your church's culture.

You live out the Circle of Tov, you practice the fruit of the Spirit, and you walk the way of Jesus. Not perfectly, but you are heading in the right direction. Your conversations over a lengthy period—enough time for the juice of ideas to ferment into a good wine—lead you to some confidence. Your coalition grows solid enough to handle negative responses or even rejections. Your ideas form into a solid core of truth. Then, and only then, are you ready to speak to those in power.

> Pockets of tov are like pockets of civil disobedience. Stephen Charles Mott lists five requirements in civil disobedience that have value for those who commit to pockets of tov. We have adjusted them for our context.
>
> 1. You oppose something wrong.
> 2. You have tried the proper paths of those in power.
> 3. You don't do this in a clandestine, deceptive manner.
> 4. You have a chance of success.
> 5. You are willing to accept the decisions of those in power.[5]

SPEAKING TO POWER

Realize what you are doing. Accept that you are essentially powerless. Prepare yourself well and schedule an appointment to meet with someone in power who you discern may have a listening ear. Again, realize that you probably will be perceived as divisive. Do whatever you can to be tov as tov can be.

If a crime has occurred, report it to the police. If it is sexual harassment in the workplace, contact the Equal Employment Opportunity Commission, the human resources department, or other appropriate authorities.

Otherwise, follow protocols and processes as much as possible. It would be wise for you to contact the person you want to speak with and say, "I have a concern about some problems I'm seeing at the church, and I wonder how I should proceed. To whom should I speak? How would you like to be approached?" I have seen some doggone good ideas scuttled because someone knocked on the wrong door too soon. You need not be in a hurry; do this right. Accept that you have no power. Don't grovel, but also don't act like you are the prophet Amos, pounding on the Temple authorities' doors.

Develop a realistic expectation for each meeting you have. Think of being heard and think of your voice being given an opportunity. At this point, you may feel satisfied that you were given an ear, that they held a meeting with you, and that you got to speak your mind.

Be patient. Don't expect a toxic culture (again, *if* you are right) to admit it's toxic. Toxicity often goes along with a total lack of self-awareness. Toxicity is as much a homeostasis as tov is. Ask for a response and ask for a time by which the powers will respond. Be flexible. Spend time in your pocket of tov in prayer, Bible study, and support of one another.

And get ready for blowback! Toxic church leaders with power will out-narrate you because they have both platform and power. They may spin some false narratives, gaslight you, and do what many today call DARVO: Deny, Attack, and Reverse the Victim and Offender. Blowback typifies the instinct of toxic powers in all institutions, including the church.

BECOMING A WHISTLEBLOWER

First, a personal story. Willow Creek's tragic abuse revelations became public in the spring of 2018. As I (Laura) struggled to make sense of the discrepancy between a church my husband and I loved and the pastor's moral failing, the stories wound their way into countless conversations with family and friends.

Inexplicably to me at the time and in the aftermath of the story unfolding, I found myself the angry target of Willow Creek employees and church members who lashed out at me for a plethora of offenses related to my public comments in defense of the abused. I must confess that I wasn't always kind and loving in my advocacy. I certainly spoke words that were too harsh and defended the victims too fiercely. Still, I struggled for months to understand people's anger toward me—rather than toward the church—and to cope with it. I mourned the loss of friendships while still believing that truth provided the only way forward and that eventually my disaffected friends would welcome it.

Only now, years later and after dozens of conversations and much research on the topic, do I understand culture's power over the people living within it. I understand now that culture gives members their identity and self-esteem and tells them how to behave and feel good about themselves. Perhaps my public comments about my deep disappointment in the church and its leadership had tread dangerously close to upending other members' self-esteem and identity.

I am not alone. In the last year, we have heard from countless whistleblowers in Christian and secular organizations. They experienced the same kind of angry attacks that I did, though the organizations, specifics, and details differ. Almost all lost relationships, as I did, mostly for speaking up and asking a church or Christian workplace to tell the truth. Some lent their names to newspaper articles and found themselves cut off from communities they loved. I cannot say with certainty that culture created my painful situation or theirs, but it is at least worth considering in light of the power we know it has.

Understand, then, that whistleblowers are never met with open, loving arms and listening ears. Your whistleblowing may forever mark you and *will* disrupt relationships—one of the common reasons people give for not speaking up.

It often goes like this: You take all the prescribed steps, the powers that be listen (or pretend to listen), nothing is done, and the toxicity remains. To get their attention, you conclude that you must do what Israel's prophets did: They took symbolic prophetic actions, walking around naked for a year, or lying flat on their side for days, or smashing pots in public spaces. But instead of some prophetic act, such as protesting with a sign outside the church entrance, you want to go public—just as the prophets did who stood in the courts of Jerusalem. We call this whistleblowing.

In most cases, whistleblowing amounts to public shaming, which can be dangerous. It should occur only after all other avenues have been attempted and blocked. We live in a country based on law, and it's civil to proceed by policies, procedures, and protocols. It is also civil to go to the authorities when appropriate.

We say all of this to emphasize that, in our outrage-and-callout culture, whistleblowing may seem to be the easier path to gain a following than doing things some other way. But it must be a late option, not an early option.

The issue is power. If toxins are coursing through a church's system, producing contaminated fruit, and if the powers that be will not listen to repeated attempts to get a hearing to make things right, then whistleblowing becomes a necessary option.

Whistleblowers do their work in several ways:

- going to the human resources department at an institution, as some of our friends have done
- speaking up in a committee to make a concern known
- filing a grievance with the church or with a lawyer in court
- using social media

Social media has the power of immediate feedback. As a radical democracy, it operates with the possibility of going viral and making a case known internationally. A fiasco related to sexual abuse in churches in Champaign, Illinois, provides one example.

Nothing happened until a victim told her story in detail on Instagram. Then another. Then another. This got the attention of the authorities. Getting public attention may prompt a church to finally pursue a genuinely tov resolution.

Churches, whether toxic or tov, crave stability. The prophets in the Bible were destabilizers. Likewise, speaking up, speaking out, and resisting toxic dimensions of a church culture is destabilizing. The stabilizers—pastors, boards, the silent majority, the unknowing—resist the destabilizers. But the prophets of tov will not tolerate toxicity in the place where God's Spirit is called to transform cultures into tov.

Our family became whistleblowers about Willow Creek in a secondary sense. I (Scot) blogged about it and spoke publicly about it in my classes and with others. Laura used her social media to "like" and tweet and make public comments. We paid for that. I paid for that. But it was worth it because we believed the women and not the church's self-protective spinning of the narrative.

Whistleblowers *always* lose reputation and status in their former groups. If you choose to use social media, even if you do it well and wisely and strategically, you will suffer a loss of friendships.

We had dinner with a couple who had become whistleblowers in a tight circle of pastors and churches. A major media outlet approached them about "going on the record"; that is, attaching their names to their observations. They asked our advice.

"It will cost you," we told them. They nodded their heads in agreement, in part because it had already cost them. But they knew that going into the print media of a major publication carried a much bigger potential cost. "But who will defend the women if you don't speak up?" I asked.

They wrote us a couple of days later that they had gone on the record. Their story worked redemptively.

DISCERNING NEXT STEPS

We've mentioned flexibility, and here it deserves a reminder. You don't know what may happen when you become a whistleblower. Probably it will cause chaos at some level. Your amygdala will start firing. You can't predict next steps, so we offer the following:

- Give yourself a schedule for how long you are willing to go back and forth with the church.
- Determine what decisions or shifts by the powers that be must be made before you can continue the pursuit of tov in this church.
- Be realistic about what changes are made.
- Realize the chances are slim that the toxic powers will change.
- Stay in your tov pocket, return to your pocket, and find fellowship there.
- If necessary, find a new church.

We are being frank. Resisting in pockets of tov may well settle into a lasting tolerance for you, or it may become an unacceptable situation. We encourage you to stay committed to doing the right thing at the right time. And then decide what to do next.

Warm Up

1. What can *you* do to help spark transformation in a toxic culture?

2. Why can culture transformation occur only if the people with power use it for transforming toward tov?

3. How many of the first five assumptions listed on page 139 are true of you? What does your answer reveal to you?

4. Do you entertain a "wishful image of pious community"? Explain.

Get Some Insight

1. List several individuals in your church or organization whom you believe could join you to form a pocket of tov.

2. On a scale of 1 to 10, how committed are you to staying in your church or organization and seeing this process through?

   1————————————5————————————10
   Not at all   Completely

3. How prepared are you for the serious blowback that will surely come your way once you confront the toxic culture?

   1————————————5————————————10
   Not at all   Completely

Do the Hard Work

Since none of us knows what may happen once we become whistle-blowers, we offer several questions for you to answer regarding how you can proceed.

1. How long are you willing to go back and forth with the church or organization? What is your timeline?

2. What decisions or shifts by the powers that be must occur before you can continue the pursuit of tov in your church or organization?

3. How can you make sure you're being realistic about the changes that are made?

4. In your situation, how realistic are the chances that the toxic powers will change?

5. What will it take for you to stay in your pocket of tov and find fellowship there, once the blowback begins?

6. If you feel the need to change churches or organizations, what candidates can you identify as a suitable landing place? What factors will you employ to make your decision?

PART 3

THREE PIVOTAL POWERS

NURTURE CONGREGATIONAL CULTURE

YOU AND I ARE NOT THE REAL AGENTS of the pivot, of any deep transformation in the church. God is. But God has chosen to work through us as co-agents in the work of transforming toxic church cultures to cultures of tov. Keep in mind that transformation will not happen until the transformers themselves have been transformed by God's gracious energies.

During the writing process, we have often discussed the order of the book's chapters. At times, almost every one of them has made its case for going first. This chapter shouted among the loudest. But we placed it here so that all that has been said (and all that will yet be said) will surround this important theme: *The work of transformation is God's work.*

Only through his power will transformation ever take place.

GOD'S WORK . . . *AND* OURS

After years of gospel work, watching community after community form from the ground up, the apostle Paul described his mission. Do you know how he described it? He pictured it as working *with* God *with* God's power. I have italicized some expressions that deserve our attention in the following passage:

> *All this is from God*, who reconciled us to himself through Christ and gave us the ministry of reconciliation: that *God was reconciling the world to himself in Christ*, not counting people's sins against them. And he has committed to us the message of reconciliation. *We are therefore Christ's ambassadors, as though God were making his appeal through us*. We implore you *on Christ's behalf*: Be reconciled to God. God made him who had no sin to be sin for us, so that *in him* we might become the righteousness *of God*.
>
> *As God's co-workers* we urge you not to receive *God's* grace in vain.
>
> 2 CORINTHIANS 5:18–6:1

Without question, it is God's job to transform your culture from toxic to tov; but you are called to participate in what God is doing by entering into his work. Not your work, not my work, but God's work. It can get a little complicated to say it this way, but the general idea is very clear: It's not us; it's God.

Still, we must not forget what Paul declared: "Through Christ . . . [God] gave us the ministry of reconciliation." God does his redemptive work in this world through Christ's death and resurrection, thus making peace between himself and humanity and between one person and another. That's God's work, and *he calls us to join him and enter into that work* by declaring what he is doing and by joining him in his ongoing work of transformation.

Knowing that God is at work both removes the burden from our shoulders and empowers us to know that God's energy, God's power, is working toward tov. Let's look briefly now at a few more Bible verses that reinforce Scripture's emphasis on transformation as *God's* work and not ours.

The gifts of the Spirit are God at work in and through us:

There are different kinds of working, but in all of them and
in everyone *it is the same God at work*. . . . All these are *the
work of one and the same Spirit*, and he distributes them to
each one, just as he determines.
1 CORINTHIANS 12:6, 11, ITALICS ADDED

In a broader sense, consider Paul's exhortation to the Ephesians:

Now to him who is able to do immeasurably more than all
we ask or imagine, *according to his power that is at work
within us*, to him be glory in the church.
EPHESIANS 3:20-21, ITALICS ADDED

Paul could gladly say to the Colossians:

So that we may present everyone fully mature in Christ . . .
I strenuously contend *with all the energy Christ so powerfully
works in me*.
COLOSSIANS 1:28-29, ITALICS ADDED

Further, as he told the Romans:

I will not venture to speak of anything except what *Christ
has accomplished through me* in leading the Gentiles to obey
God by what I have said and done—by the power of signs
and wonders, *through the power of the Spirit of God*. So
from Jerusalem all the way around to Illyricum, *I have fully
proclaimed* the gospel of Christ.
ROMANS 15:18-19, ITALICS ADDED

And he could tell the Christians at Corinth:

By the grace of God I am what I am, and his grace to me was
not without effect. No, *I worked harder than all of them*—yet
not I, *but the grace of God was with me*.
1 CORINTHIANS 15:10, ITALICS ADDED

So, let's review:

God is at work.
God calls *you* into that work.
And *God* is at work *in you* and *through you* as *his coworker*.

Though God is always at work in many ways, in part 3 we want to draw your attention to three of the main pivotal powers he uses. These energize us as we work with God to transform a toxic church's culture. This chapter focuses on what we can do, through God's Spirit, to nurture congregational culture. Chapter 10 focuses on how we can rely on the Holy Spirit to move a culture toward tov. And chapter 11 highlights the key role of God's grace in making everything tov happen.

CONGREGATIONAL CULTURE IS A POWER?

It might surprise you to learn that the first kind of power God uses in transformation is *congregational culture*. Some may well moan and groan at this point, because for them the congregation is the *problem*! We are on board with you.

It helps to remember that groups matter immensely for forming culture and for assimilating people into a culture. Corrupted groups can corrupt both the culture and the people in it. You may have witnessed the anger of a church or institution toward whistleblowers for going public about what those with power considered internal matters. In many of these situations, those who went public had worked hard internally to gain some attention for their concerns. But as long as the power remained in the hands of corrupted leaders, the concerns of the whistleblowers were suppressed. So when the whistleblowers went public, the powerful grew angry and lashed out at those calling attention to serious concerns.

Notice that something *in the culture* prompted those with power to act as they did toward the truth-telling whistleblowers. Instead of facing the truth, repenting, and growing into God's gracious work of redemption, they were constrained by the culture itself to fight against the truth.

With that in mind, let's try to understand how a culture forms into an active agent. The theory works like this:

- Practices and acts form into habits.
- Habits form into a culture agent (a group taking on the power to influence).
- The culture agent acts upon humans to conform to the culture.
- We practice habits that deepen the culture.
- And around and around we go in the same direction.[1]

This all means that the congregation is an agent of culture influence, formation, and transformation. If the culture brims with toxins, such as having a desire for fame, glory, and money, the congregation will distort people away from Christlikeness. If the culture is tov, the congregation will shape toward tov.

AN ILLUSTRATION OF CHURCH POWER

Consider one example of how a church's toxic practices communicate a culture. I (Laura) attended Willow Creek for nearly two decades. During that time I met senior pastor Bill Hybels twice—once when he baptized me on stage, and once when I waited in line to meet him after a weekend service. During my time at Willow, I never had the expectation of talking to Hybels or for him to know me or even recognize my face. After all, Willow was a megachurch that drew enormous weekend crowds, and Bill Hybels walked around the campus with a bodyguard after every service. I remember a handful of times (or fewer) when I saw him in the lobby after a Saturday evening service. Truth be told, on those rare occasions I behaved as if I'd sighted a Hollywood celebrity. Remember, both the congregation and the leadership are agents that actively influence one another and define the culture. So there I would stand gaping, treating Hybels like the celebrity he was.

The larger point is this: Congregants rarely saw Bill Hybels on campus after services, and when they did, he would be with an entourage that discouraged them from speaking to him. He had his own garage and private entrance at the church. The church maintained an elaborate backstage space, including a greenroom, allowing those on stage to comfortably retreat from the congregation.

Now, years removed from attending Willow Creek (and perhaps with a keener ability to evaluate culture), I see how their physical space spoke to me of *status*. It spoke of *inaccessibility* and *fame* and *you're-not-important-enough*. It separated the haves from the have-nots, the in-crowd from the rest. It was a platform designed for a celebrity culture.

I'm no longer a part of Willow Creek, so I cannot evaluate its current physical space. Perhaps it has changed, perhaps not. But during my two decades at the church, I remember feeling less important than those on stage, in large part (I think) due to how the physical layout created separation and expressed a celebrity culture.

Contrast this well-known example with a church culture designed to truly welcome people. What would those facilities look like?

To begin with, the atmosphere would be *worshipful*. By this I mean a space that is welcoming to all; that provides the information each person needs in order to participate; that is designed so that each person seated can see the leaders on the platform. Further, it has leaders who genuinely lead people to understand what worship is and how singing and listening and praying are all elements of worship; leaders who make people feel comfortable with their style of participation (sitting, standing, raising hands, not raising hands, etc.—you know what I mean).

Second, it would be designed for *fellowship*. Does that mean the seating would be arranged in rows, all aimed at the pulpit or altar? How can we create a feeling of fellowship if we can't see each other's faces?

I (Laura) wandered into many a Twitter conversation in recent years. Twitter's call-out and cancel culture can at times be brutal, and I'm sorry to say that too often I participate. Yet one morning I found the gentle tweets of a Quaker pastor named Scott Wagoner, whose demeanor was so gracious and opposite of what so often prevails on social media. Wagoner posts a centering prayer every morning and evening—prayers that he writes himself—and I find his soulful tweets restorative as my days begin and end. What I found especially striking one day (February 3, 2022) was a photo Wagoner posted of his church's chapel space. I almost gaped as I took in the worship space, the benches *in a circle*.

Those attending the worship service would see *one another,* I thought, *and no one is elevated in importance because no one speaks from a platform.* The contrast was so striking because I have only ever attended churches where pastors speak from a stage or a platform.

Perhaps the Quakers are on to something, I thought.

Kris and I (Scot) once took a tour of Israel. During our flight home, somewhere between Greenland and Canada, with five or six people from our tour group around me, I looked out a window to see what looked like confetti all over the blue ocean. It dawned on me that I was seeing melting icebergs bobbing along.

"Wow, global warming," I said aloud. My words prompted some irritated facial expressions, as if the individuals were muttering to themselves, *You don't believe in that nonsense, do you?*

Our group had been together for almost two weeks, and we had gotten to know one another. But I felt tension in that moment with a culture at work. Call it what you want—social pressure or culture—but some kind of "agent" was telling me to get in line. I didn't, but later I described the encounter to Kris, who said, "Really? Maybe they should have a conversation with the folks in Greenland."

This is a small example, but if one were to buckle under that kind of social constraint to keep out of trouble, one would soon get in the habit of denying global warming—and the more who live under that buckle, the more powerful that culture becomes.

Groups matter.

THE POWER OF GROUPS

All groups have power. Think of the cutthroat culture of a Wall Street investment firm; the tense culture at Apple when Steve Jobs was being Steve Jobs; the pressure to silence (especially female) whistle-blowers in the news media; the lack of human wisdom at work in some cultures of our social media landscape. Or just think of the Netflix documentary *The Social Dilemma*, which looks at the power of social media to manipulate group attitudes and behaviors.[2] Think of these places as cultures that shape those who inhabit them.

Do you think such cultures have power?

One pastor described his former working environment to us: "The church's culture reinforced your behavior and then blessed you or punished you depending on your interaction with it."

Listen to David Brooks, a columnist for the *New York Times*: "Never underestimate the power of the environment you work in to gradually transform who you are. When you choose to work at a certain company, you are turning yourself into the sort of person who works in that company."[3] The same could be said about the churches where we choose to worship. If Brooks is right (and we are convinced that he is), then we must begin right here: The first energy source in transforming a culture is the *cultural power of the congregation* to mold us into "those who fit in."

I (Scot) am a theologian, so let me explain this differently. The Spirit of God works on us to transform us from toxic humans into tov humans. The Spirit works to form us, not just as individuals, but also as a church. The Spirit wants us to be the body of Christ. The more Spirit-prompted tov we do together, the more tov our culture becomes. The more tov our culture becomes, the more "pressure" is applied on everyone to act in tov ways.

There's more to think about here. Consider this: *The single most common way any person meets Christ is through other people.* Jesus called his followers "the salt of the earth" and "the light of the world" (Matthew 5:13-16). God has called us, Paul said, to be human agents of reconciliation (2 Corinthians 5:16-21). Paul tells us in Romans 15:16 that he himself is a priestly mediator of the gospel. You and I are mediators of God's redemption in our world. We are agents for God. That's our calling. That's how God has chosen to spread the gospel in our world.

It's also how God has chosen to transform toxic cultures into tov cultures.

Now the strongest statement of all: *Congregations mediate, or connect us to, God, the transforming God.* This mediation, of course, doesn't occur infallibly. Neither will the mediation that occurs look entirely tov. But congregations do mediate. A church relates a message about God, it embodies that message—sometimes well, sometimes not—and that message and embodiment together communicate (mediate) God to us. We experience God by how our congregations communicate God to us.

Congregations mediate culture. Tov congregations mediate tov; toxic congregations mediate toxicity.

Your church mediates God to the people influenced and affected by your church. When congregations become tov, they can become an energy source to transform congregants into tov-ness and tov-hood (to invent some terms). To change a church culture requires a congregation to learn new habits and new practices so that they develop a new culture. Only then can they mediate tov to everyone in the congregation. We need to learn to trust the power of a congregation to shape people toward tov character transformation.

UNDERSTANDING COMES FIRST

Transforming a church culture into a tov culture must link tightly to tov character. But this requires us to understand our culture; that is, that we must get deep into the soil to discover what drives the energies of that culture.

We've already heard several times from John Rosensteel, who formerly pastored in Madison, Wisconsin. While there, Blackhawk Church mushroomed from four hundred to four thousand in attendance. Flourishing sometimes rouses the Spirit to move people on, and God led John and his wife, Corrie, to New Hope Church in Portland, Oregon. New Hope, one of the first megachurches in the United States, began at a drive-in theater (like Robert Schuller's famous Crystal Cathedral) and eventually topped out at an attendance of five thousand people. That attendance boom encouraged New Hope to build a massive facility that could house even more growth, but it led instead to financial stress.

By the time John arrived as New Hope's pastor, attendance had dwindled to 1,200, with a building and mortgage far too big for the congregation and a facility in need of much more than love. As John tells it, "Cash reserves were meager and giving was trending downward. Staff morale was low. Division and gossip were rampant."

With a little bit of hope offsetting some toxicity that lay deeper in the soil than they realized, the leaders wondered whether New Hope could be revitalized with a remodel. They soon discovered the answer: No. John said it this way: "Unhealthy cultures aren't rooted out in one season. A trusted mentor who had experience in changing culture at numerous organizations told me it would take seven years, although he said we would begin to see and feel change after three. Though I inwardly scoffed at those time estimates, he was spot on."[4]

John and New Hope learned together that the church's soil needed a lot of work. It took some honest evaluation to fully comprehend the church's culture. They learned of fractured relationships, some distortions of power, and some ineffective shapes of communication, miscommunication, and lack of communication. They learned they needed a new vision and mission, a fresher theology, and some new faces among the leaders.

LEARN YOUR INSTITUTION'S HISTORY

Part of the process of honest culture evaluation requires looking back at your church's history. A newly hired pastor may feel tempted to say, "That happened when I wasn't here. That's not my sin to own." But this invites problems because the past still affects the current culture. The past makes up part of the peach tree's shape and health; the past feeds its roots and transportation systems; and the past remains in the soil. One pastor told us that he and his team read one chapter per week of *A Church Called Tov*, followed by discussions that centered entirely around grappling with the church's past.

Culture transformation requires a leadership willing to hear about pain in the past and willing to commit to its redemption. You must make such a commitment even if you didn't work on staff when the problems developed, because those problems still lie hidden in the active parts of your culture. They don't just disappear when new faces come on board. The new leader must uncover and learn what is producing the peach tree's toxic blossoms and diseased fruit. It is the new leader's responsibility to listen and learn and respond wisely and compassionately.

AN INSTRUMENT FOR DISCOVERING YOUR CHURCH'S CULTURE

One day a pastor friend called me (Scot). He had read *A Church Called Tov* and really liked it. He asked, "Do you have an assessment tool for the book?"

"No," I answered, "but we need one." So Laura and I, along with others, have worked to create the Tov Tool found in the appendix. It provides a series of questions designed for staff members (all of whom are promised safety) to discuss in small groups. We want to help churches develop conversations that lead to discovery, so they can start moving toward a tov culture.

We know what you might be muttering right about now: "*I don't feel safe answering questions about our church's culture.*" That problem needs to be addressed at another level. For now, we will sketch out for you the Tov Tool.

Asking good questions, discussing responses in safety and candor, and participating in the insights of new discoveries all promote comprehension of one's church culture. Taking a survey can help, but we believe that open-ended conversations in a safe environment will lead to significant discoveries about the DNA of your culture. This cannot happen without note-taking, reliable reporting, and receptive listening. We pray that the Tov Tool will help you begin to come to terms with your church's culture.

Wise church leaders may want to ponder just one question per month, because follow-ups and further conversations will need to happen. We break down the use of the Tov Tool into three phases; but please consider these only as suggestions, based on what we have learned from those who have worked at transforming cultures. What matters most is conversation and discovery. Your phases may well differ from the three suggested.

Phase 1: Questions, Conversations, Discoveries

You can use the Tov Tool either in its entirety or section by section. We designed it to generate both conversation and discovery among people who feel safe with one another.

For you to accurately discern your culture and learn the truth, you will need to ask questions in a safe context. You must also make sure that someone's honest answers do not become the source of recriminations. We should tell you up front that this tool has *not* been validated by psychologists who study toxic cultures, nor is it a normed survey.

The first, last, and most important evaluation question is this: *How central is Jesus—his life, his teachings, his death, his glory—to your church and institution?* Is he often talked about? Is he the Presence in every room and conversation and program? In other words, how Christlike is your church, your institution, your Christian business? In what ways are your people like Christ and in what ways are they not?

The Tov Tool has six sections. In the first, we ask questions about *empathy* such as this one: Are people of color treated with empathy? The answers that matter most here will come from people of color. Empathy is the capacity to understand other people in their pain or joy, to enter into their pain or joy, and to experience it with them as an act of love and for the purpose of caring for them well.

Tov people and tov churches also exhibit the character trait of *grace*. Because they have received a great gift through which a new relationship has formed, they respond with gratitude and offer gifts back to the giver, which helps to form them into agents of grace. So we ask questions such as, "Is God's grace trusted enough to permit people to grow in Christ and in their gifts and skills?"

What we call "institution creep" provides one of the quickest indicators of a toxic church culture. In such an environment, the institution and its reputation matter more than any person (other than the pastor and those in his inner circle, unfortunately). Indicators include rapid departures of employees without explanation, the requirement to sign non-disparagement agreements, and running roughshod over the feelings and emotions of workers and friends of those workers. Perhaps most of all, workers have the sense that "you can't fight city hall" (as we say here in Chicagoland). Questions like this can expose the need for a church to grow in valuing *people first*: Do those above you and around you know your name, your family members, your story?

Perhaps the single most shocking discovery we have made in this new ministry of ours to people suffering from church abuse comes down to the false narratives created by churches to protect the pastors, the staff, and the church. Too often, the institution matters more than *truth telling*.

Our litigious society has swallowed up the church's requirement to tell the truth. We have no beef with lawyers per se, but we also know that churches bent on spinning the narrative protect themselves by appealing to lawyers, who think about lawsuits more than truth telling. Consider one good question to begin a discussion: Is your church or institution characterized by people who ignore reality, even though the reality of some truth is known and knowable? Such a serious problem can damage the character, the very soil, of your church. The Bible tells us that the father of lies is the evil one (John 8:44).

To pursue a tov culture in your organization means that it both espouses and embodies the value of *justice*. We can easily get off track here and begin thinking the term *justice* derives from the US Constitution or the Bill of Rights, but the Christian value comes from the Bible's consistent teaching that we measure justice by the character of God and God's revealed will. In essence, *justice* means "doing the right thing" and implies, often enough, "at the right time."

Toxic church cultures demand loyalty and blind trust of power leaders, who seem to think only they can determine what is just. They imply that only their decisions measure justice! Here is a hard question to ask of your church: Is your church characterized by people for whom loyalty transcends doing the right thing at the right time? Or rephrased, have you ever asked someone to do something wrong because it would benefit the system?

Let's say it again: The essence of Christlikeness is for everyone to use whatever power they have for the good of others instead of just for themselves. In a word, such people are known for their *service*. Treating a spiritual leader as a mediator of God's grace to you and to me colors between the lines of all churches. Turning such leaders into celebrities hops the lines and sets off warning bells. The pastor becomes one who must be served and coddled and protected, rather than being a servant. Tov churches are characterized by the character trait of service. Here is one question that opens the door to the church's culture: Is your institution characterized by people above you and around you who expect to be served? Or said differently, Is service expected or demanded in ways that degrade, shame, or are otherwise inappropriate?

The Tov Tool has a bundle of questions around each of the six topics just mentioned. We believe these questions can open up the possibility of discovering the profile of a church's culture.

Phase 2: Discoveries, Assessment, Planning an Approach

After your church begins to discover major elements of the church's culture by asking questions, the time has come for wise people to assess those discoveries. We recommend assigning your culture a grade for each of the six sections, assuming that the six add up to an all-important Christlikeness grade.

Don't quantify your results too much, because quantified numbers—such as, "We are an 89 on service"—tend to produce a false objectivity. Give yourself rounded grades: A, B, C, and "We have lots of work to do." (Grade inflation in our culture means we can no longer assign grades below a C.)

We suggest you order the topics by grades, like this:

Service, Justice: A
Empathy, Grace: B
People First, Truth Telling: C

By this point, you have isolated some dimensions of your culture that need more work than others. Now start planning an approach to ameliorate *one* of these dimensions. Let's say that your low grade for *people first* surprised you. You learn that many staff members feel ignored or unknown, and that their wishes and wills are overpowered by those above them. You learn that women are not being treated with dignity and respect. You therefore decide to tackle that dimension of your church first.

Phase 3: Questions, Conversations, Discoveries

Think of phase 3 as a "rinse and repeat" stage. Good organizations strive for ongoing health, which means they commit themselves to ongoing assessments of progress and regress. Not only will good churches assess how *people first* progress is going, but they will continue to monitor that progress for new discoveries and new areas of needed improvement.

At Oak Hills Church, Kent Carlson and Mike Lueken began to see their church as an "open laboratory" where they could continue to learn and grow and adjust.[5] Their book *Renovation of the Church* could carry the subtitle: *And Our Commitment to Continual Renovation.*

> Transformation will not happen until the transformers themselves are transformed by God's gracious power.

Ongoing conversations and discoveries must happen if a church wants to transform itself into a character-shaped (tov-shaped) culture. Easier desired than done! The Tov Tool can help you develop a plan for creating a healthier culture that practices genuine transformation.

A SIGHTING OF TRANSCENDENCE

I (Laura) recently received a letter from a pastor of a multiethnic church who told me they have begun a period of soul-searching. He described a desire for a tov culture, one free of sexism, sexual harassment, and abuse. Deeply affected by a region-wide revelation of abuse and mistreatment of women, and the church's own role in that culture, the entire church community has started to reflect on women's roles, gender, and how the church treats women.

When I visited this church, I witnessed something transcendent: a wonderful willingness to learn, to ask questions, and to seriously reflect on the reality of the church culture. I saw a surrendering to truth, a commitment to conversation, a desire to work with God however God might call them to this work of transformation. I witnessed a godly surrender in the senior pastor, in his wife, and in volunteers and congregants. The reality of tov creation felt contagious. I witnessed a growing coalition and saw the congregation participating. Most of all, I observed the transcendent working of the Spirit of God in this church.

One step at a time.

Warm Up

1. How has God called you into the work of transformation at your church or organization?

2. How have you seen God's grace at work in your life as an agent of transformation?

3. What one word would you use to describe the kind of power most often exercised in your church or organization? Explain why you chose this word.

Get Some Insight

1. What do you know of the history of your church or organization? Summarize it.

2. How does the history of your church or organization help you to understand its current typical exercise of power?

3. Carefully consider the following "Twelve Temptations to Avoid" before you start using the Tov Tool:

   a. *Avoid trying to transform your culture* without first doing exhaustive, careful planning of theology, procedures, and prayer, plus pondering and waiting (and waiting) in patience for what God might work next.

   b. *Avoid believing you can plan, orchestrate, and control* your desired outcome with exactitude. Planned churches, like planned societies, require coercion and tyranny.

   c. *Avoid reducing the pool of active agents to a limited number of friends.* You will discover the most surprising suggestions from people you didn't expect.

   d. *Avoid thinking the church is yours.* It's not. It is the body of Christ and it belongs to Christ. Not only is the church not yours, it is the entire congregation's and likely existed before you arrived. And it will likely exist after you leave.

e. *Avoid using agitation* as a motivator for change or transformation.

f. *Avoid utopian thinking*, which means avoid believing that if everyone in the church jumps aboard your bandwagon, you will usher everyone into the millennium or some idealized kingdom right now. You are convinced and passionate and have expectations and hopes, but get real: This side of the New Jerusalem, your church, at its best, will still be full of sinners.

g. *Avoid taking the bull by the horns, thinking you can wrestle the church culture to the ground*, and that, when you pin it to the floor, it will yell "Uncle!" and give up and do things your way.

h. *Avoid becoming the very problem—coercive powers—you are trying to change.* You want to change a culture only because something has gone wrong with it, and the something wrong is *always* connected to power. Avoid misusing power.

i. *Avoid firing everyone who doesn't agree with you.* Or putting such persons in positions on staff so they will quit. Or shaming people into feeling uncomfortable enough to walk away. Or creating a gossip mill about so-and-so and did-you-hear-this-about-her threads.

j. *Avoid believing you can just preach a sermon series, along with creating some home Bible studies to supplement and support the series, and so transform the culture.* A few times in church history someone preached a single sermon or a series and the culture of a place changed. That's true about them, but not for you. Forget it.

k. *Avoid launching a program or initiative because you want your church to address a particular issue.* Deciding that your culture doesn't encompass diversity and then launching a diversity program will not transform the culture. Consider the possibility that you don't have a social justice program because the culture in your church doesn't *want* one or is not the kind of culture that produces such activism.

l. *Avoid thinking that ridding the church of a particular narcissist will clear the toxins and create a tov culture.* It might become part of the process, but it's not a guarantee.

Do the Hard Work

1. Carefully review our summary of the Tov Tool on pages 163–168.

2. With a small group of individuals invested in the health of your church or organization, use the Tov Tool in the appendix to begin assessing the culture of your church or organization. Consider taking the survey over a long, set period of time in order to encourage plenty of discussion and conversation.

10

RELY ON THE HOLY SPIRIT

SOME OF US TEND TO TRIP over something in the Bible. The apostle Paul, in his letter to the Romans, says:

> There is no one righteous, not even one;
>> there is no one who understands;
>> there is no one who seeks God.
> All have turned away,
>> they have together become worthless;
> there is no one who does good,
>> not even one.
> Their throats are open graves;
>> their tongues practice deceit.
> The poison of vipers is on their lips.
>> Their mouths are full of cursing and bitterness.
> Their feet are swift to shed blood;
>> ruin and misery mark their ways,
> and the way of peace they do not know.
>> There is no fear of God before their eyes.

ROMANS 3:10-18

You can be excused if you think Paul somehow had a bad night of sleep after spending the afternoon in the hot sun running away from his opponents. Reading from top to bottom, these words sound nothing short of pessimistic. Never mind that he picked this up from Psalm 14:1-3 or Psalm 53:2-4. It's still wholly negative. Yes, Paul's got himself into a logical argument in which he wants to make it clear that everybody's so guilty of sin that nobody can even *be* tov or *do* tov.

So we ask him, with some hesitation: "There's *no one* who does good?"

Paul: "*Not even one.*"

You can list your "What about so-and-so?" and we can list ours (Mr. Rogers, our friends Laurie Nelson and Jaime Patrick). But let's think about this: The man who said, "There is no one who does good" in Romans 3:12 is the very same individual who wrote to the Galatians that one of the peach-tree fruits of the Spirit was nothing other than . . . wait for it . . . *goodness* (Galatians 5:22).

So how do we put this together?

On our own, as unredeemed sinners, as people of the flesh, *not one of us* is capable of doing good or of being good. We could perhaps squeeze out a little virtue and say that with sufficient willpower and discipline and practice we could get better. But according to the psalmist and the apostle Paul, we will never ever be good all on our own.

GOD IN US

If you have placed your faith in Jesus as your Lord and Savior, then you are no longer an unredeemed sinner, a person ruled by the flesh. In fact, Scripture insists that because Christ has redeemed you, *God now indwells you by the Spirit.* This changes everything . . . but not necessarily all at once.

It's not like a fleshly guy turns his life over to Jesus, gets filled with the Spirit, and that night goes home fully sanctified, totally loving, and onward and upward toward perfection he goes. No, it's not like that.

It takes reading only a few pages of the Gospels, where we see the disciples fail, or a quick reading of the letters of Paul, where we encounter one moral problem after another among the early Christians, to see the error in that idea. No, having the Holy Spirit in our lives doesn't mean automatic spiritual formation and maturity.

But *God in us by the Spirit* matters much.

CHRIST IN US

So convinced is Paul of God's presence within us that his language gets a bit confusing. To begin with, we are "in Christ" (or the Lord), or "in him." The first version occurs more than eighty times in Paul's letters. A perfect verse to illustrate the "in him" idea says, "So then, just as you received Christ Jesus as *Lord*, continue to live your lives *in him*, rooted and built up *in him*, strengthened in the faith as you were taught, and overflowing with thankfulness" (Colossians 2:6-7, italics added).

To make sure we don't miss the profundity of what this verse says (because of our familiarity with it), consider another of the apostle's startling assertions: "In Christ all the fullness of the Deity lives in bodily form, and in Christ you have been brought to fullness" (Colossians 2:9-10).

Notice two things here.

First, the fullness of what makes God *God* lives in Jesus.

Second, we are "in Christ," and in Christ we have been "brought" into the "fullness" that makes God who he is. It's more than we can possibly comprehend.

But at least we can understand this much: We are in Christ, Christ is God, and by entering into Christ, we brush up against the fullness of God. And so, we have entered the circle called "God/Christ." (If you want a few more Bible verses about being "in Christ," look up Romans 8:1; 1 Corinthians 1:2; and especially 2 Corinthians 5:17: "If anyone is in Christ, the new creation has come: The old has gone, the new is here!")

US IN GOD

Do you get the picture so far? That's good, but if you move just a little further down the track, you'll find that things get a bit more confusing.

Not only are we "in" Christ, but Christ and the Spirit are "in" us! It sounds something like overlapping parts of a Venn diagram: One circle is Christ while another circle is Us. And where they intersect is where Christ and Us "live in" each other.

Now, what can all this mean? And how can coming to understand it a bit more clearly help us to live more tov-like lives?

Let's return to Paul's letter to the Colossians to see if we can find some assistance there. Near the end of the first chapter, Paul describes the gospel as the disclosed mystery of redemption for both Jews and Gentiles. Paul declares that this mystery is "Christ *in you*, the hope of glory" (Colossians 1:27, italics added).

And then there's Galatians 2:20, which reads, "I have been crucified with Christ and I no longer live, but Christ lives *in me*" (italics added).

Paul also asked a simple question of the Corinthians: "Do you not realize that Christ Jesus is *in you*?" (2 Corinthians 13:5, italics added).

And now to the important connection. To the Romans, Paul said, "If Christ is *in you*, then even though your body is subject to death because of sin, *the Spirit gives life* because of righteousness" (Romans 8:10, italics added). Here's the connection: Christ is in us *and* the Spirit is in us.

As we've already seen, we cannot transform our churches by our own power. We are indwelled by God—Christ, the Spirit—and because God is in us and at work in us and through us, transformation can occur.

We could call this a *mutual indwelling*. While this sounds wonderful, we will help ourselves the most if we think of it this way: God's Spirit is in *us as the body of Christ* and only because we are in the body of Christ is *Christ in us personally*.

THE PROBLEM WITH MODERNITY

Let's all take a deep breath and admit something: We moderns (yes, this is about modernity and not the first-century world) think first of ourselves individualistically, and only secondarily do we think of ourselves as part of a nation, state, community, or local church. While this is not good, it is very, very modern. Modernity gave rise to the *self* becoming central.

So the "God in us/us in God" mutual indwelling is about our life *as a church*, as the local body of Christ, before it is about you and me growing spiritually as individuals.

Herein lies the foundation of a huge energy source for church transformation. That power works itself out in the Bible in the fruit of the Spirit and the gifts of the Spirit.

We've already considered what Paul calls "the fruit of the Spirit," but let's go a bit deeper. Paul's wonderful letter to the Galatians can come at us like water from a fire hose if we don't take care as we read it. The apostle explains to the Galatian believers that they are in a battle between the flesh and the Spirit (Galatians 5:16-26).

The flesh, to use our terms, produces toxins such as ambition and a desire for success, money, power, glory, and fame. The Spirit, again to use our terms, produces tov. Paul calls the produce of the Spirit in our lives *fruit*. In this context, fruit is about character formation, both as a group and as individuals.

We can't conquer the flesh by our own efforts. We can't tame it, domesticate it, or make it into a nice little pet. When we attempt to defeat the flesh on our own, we tend to produce toxins that spoil the fruit.

In the power of the Spirit, however, we can be transformed from no-good to good, from no-tov to tov (hat tip to Hosea 1:2–2:1). The Spirit produces healthy fruit in us because that's what the Spirit does! The apostle Paul sincerely believes that God's Spirit not only lives in us and we in the Spirit, and that Christ lives in us and we in Christ, *but he also sincerely believes that the Spirit who lives in us can transform us*. We base this conviction not only on Galatians 5:22-23 but also on 2 Corinthians:

> Now the Lord is the Spirit, and where the Spirit of the Lord is, there is freedom. *And we all, who with unveiled faces*

contemplate the Lord's glory, are being transformed into his
image with ever-increasing glory, which comes from the
Lord, who is the Spirit.
2 CORINTHIANS 3:17-18, ITALICS ADDED

The Spirit in us sets us free as we contemplate the words, works, majesty, and power of the Lord Jesus. That contemplation of Christ, and the freedom we receive through the Spirit, enables us to say, "we all . . . are being transformed into his image." Paul declares that God's Spirit can transform our character from its natural, fleshly ways to instead adopt and embody the ways of the Spirit.

The Spirit—again, the Spirit who indwells us—is a Spirit who transforms us by prompting us to live in the way of tov. He incessantly labors as our internal monitor, pointing out sins and pointing us toward the fruit of the Spirit. But the Spirit does more than work daily on our character. The Spirit makes us *somebody* in the body of Christ.

WHAT AM I EVEN DOING HERE?

After the October 2020 publication of *A Church Called Tov*, my father and I (Laura) received an influx of requests for interviews, webinar appearances, and speaking events. To date, I believe we've collectively participated in more than 150 of these sorts of ministry-related tov events—a very high number for someone like me who has never received training in anything ministry-related. Thus I often have what I call "What am I even doing here?" moments in the middle of such events.

Whether it's a book club visit, a speaking engagement, or a podcast interview, I can begin to feel extremely out of place. Someone might ask me, for example, "Laura, how does loyalty to a leader interfere with justice?" or, "Laura, can you tell us about a power-through-fear culture, or how an abuser flips the script and presents himself or herself as the victim?"

I have these "What am I even doing here?" moments because I

am not a trained theologian. I have been trained as an educator and have spent two decades of my career as a public school teacher of young children. In fact, I am currently teaching kindergarten, which may be my favorite grade of all. During interviews about the book, therefore, I often have moments when I wonder, *Does this person not realize that I am a grade school teacher and have never worked in a church or any sort of ministry, or that I spent my day preparing ready-for-kindergarten confetti?*

I once described my personal disorientation in a podcast interview. The episode we recorded that day still lives in my memory as "The One in Which They Ministered to Me." I was invited to a live *Inverse Podcast* recording with Jarrod McKenna and Dr. Drew Hart in May 2022 on a show titled, "Laura Barringer on Clergy Abuse." I explained how I am a grade school teacher and never planned to write a book about abuse and toxicity in churches or about how to resist both. I never planned to spend my school breaks and evenings and weekends talking about these topics. At the beginning, I didn't even know what *tov* meant. I never once planned to land in this unexpected place.

But I came to feel as if I had something stirring inside me that needed to be said, and that God in his grace was prompting me to speak up and speak out. Only by God's grace did my father and I fall into this project, and only by God's grace am I able to answer these questions. And only by God's grace have I acquired the ability to speak passionately about these issues.

Jarrod McKenna suggested that my experience educating young children has provided me with a different lens through which to view this difficult topic. He labeled my writing and speaking as *advocacy* and noted my solidarity with those who suffer in toxic environments. My background as a teacher, he said, matters because theological institutions such as churches and seminaries are often sick. "You are taught to care for little ones," he said, "and those skills are more appropriate for a pastor than what is often valued in churches." His words declared to me, *God is with us and in us by his Spirit.*

Our podcast conversation provided me with a spiritual moment, an awakening of sorts, a glimpse of how the Spirit guides us from within. The Spirit can guide even a *schoolteacher* to speak into a *church abuse* crisis!

The Spirit, in fact, uses all of us in the body of Christ for his redemptive purposes. Each of us contributes to a larger transformation. Only by his grace and through his gifts can I speak and write what I do. As a primary agent of God's grace in our lives, the Spirit empowers us all to effectively exercise what we usually call "the gifts of the Spirit."

THE GIFTS: OUR CONTRIBUTION

Paul uses the phrase "gifts of the Spirit" to describe your contribution, my contribution, and all of our contributions to the mission of the gospel. Paul talks about these gifts in three passages: Romans 12:6-8; 1 Corinthians 12:1-11; and Ephesians 4:11-13. In these places he uses various names to describe the gifts, such as different kinds of "service" or "workings" or "manifestations" or "powers." Unlike us, he doesn't lock down on just one term (as we do when we speak of them only as "gifts"). If we add them all up, we find close to twenty named spiritual manifestations in these three passages; but we may misunderstand them if we aggregate them in this way. Paul shifts his terms a bit across the three letters, and this shifting indicates something vital for us to understand today.

We don't need to sort out the list and say, "Which one do I have?" Instead, we ought to ask, "How can I contribute to my local body?" The answer to that question is your gift, service, working, power, or manifestation. It's what the Spirit is doing *through you* for the good of your local body of Christ.

A friend of ours told us about a time when he accompanied the late Stuart Briscoe to a speaking engagement. At the end of Stuart's talk, an eager young man came bustling up to him, anxiously wanting to know how he could "discover" his "spiritual gift." Stuart smiled and replied in his very English way, "So you want to know what your spiritual gift is? I shall tell you. Try to do something to help someone in your community. If you can do it, you've got it. If you can't, you don't. That's it." The startled young man went away a bit sad, our friend reported—he probably wanted to know which gift inventory to take, or what seminar to attend, or what book to read—but Stuart had tried to teach him a crucial lesson. We "discover" our giftings by serving others, especially in the church. And what we do well, *voilà*! There's our gifting.

The Spirit is at work in each of us, which is why Paul sometimes calls the gifts a "working." The Spirit also prompts us to help others in our church, which is why at other times the apostle calls it a "service." But the rock-bottom reality is that whatever we contribute, we do so because we have a "gift" granted to us by the God/Christ/Spirit who indwells us.

YOU'RE ON A MISSION

You are on a mission to transform the culture of your institution. You may hope to make a big shift (from toxic to tov), or a less-than-big shift (friendlier greeters, kinder relations in some departments). The Bible insists that *you cannot make it happen*. If you try to coerce it, it will backfire. Any change *you* produce will be thinner than the skin on a peach.

You can't do it.

But God can.

A pastor friend told me (Scot) about the successful transformation of major pockets within his church. "How?" I asked him.

"All I can say," he replied, "is the Holy Spirit. It was otherwise impossible."

What can we do to gain the power of the Spirit? We must be open to the Spirit in asking and receptive prayer, in listening, in daily decisions, in routine relationships, and in major moves. We need to get our radar up and ready. If we can admit that none of us is good—no, not one—and if we can admit that the Spirit produces good fruit, then we can admit that we can move from "no one is good" to "goodness" by making ourselves receptive to the transforming work of God's good Spirit in us.

Dallas Willard developed a theory of transformation he dubbed VIM: *vision, intention*, and *means* (spiritual disciplines). In my (Scot's) book *Open to the Spirit*, I suggest a variation of Willard's theory that I dubbed VOS: *vision, openness, Spirit*.[1] I wanted to emphasize the power of the Spirit in transformation, but otherwise our approaches are nearly identical. When I asked one of Dallas's friends about my suggestion, he said, "Dallas would agree—as he taught that too!"

SYSTEMIC PROBLEMS, SYSTEMIC SOLUTIONS?

A common line these days goes like this: *systemic problems require systemic solutions*. This saying is catchier than it is accurate.

Not only is coming up with solutions easier said than done, but human systems aren't swappable. Human systems are cultures, like an orchard of peach trees, that form over time. We need reborn people beginning to do reborn practices, as the church mentioned earlier in the chapter did, one step at a time.

People are reborn by God's Spirit, not by swapping systems. People become tov by God's Spirit, not by swapping habits. On the peach tree grow peaches, and on the tree of the church grow the fruit of the Spirit, not the fruit of me or of you or even of us. No! The fruit are *of the Spirit*.

Which means we need to let go and let the Spirit of God go to work.

WHAT GOD WANTS US TO BE

We assume that most of our readers are not old enough to remember Ray Stedman, so let me set the context. Before the late 1960s and early 1970s, evangelical Christians did not talk much about the gifts of the Spirit. That language was mainly among the Pentecostals (before the charismatic movement took root among evangelicals).

Add to this what many today call cessationism, the belief that once the original apostles died, so did the need for spiritual gifts. (I'm not kidding.) The occasional Pentecostal claimed all the gifts, but by and large, this group remained outside the circle of evangelicals.

Add to this that Dispensationalists joined the Reformed to create a widespread belief in cessationism among America's evangelicals.

Now let's take a quick trip to California. In the late 1960s and early 1970s, we heard about a powerful revival among the state's youth in what came to be called the Jesus People movement. One of my (Scot's) hometown friends landed right in the middle of it, and he sometimes returned home to tell me all about it. The Jesus People not only read their Bibles and marked them up, but they believed their Bibles and tried to practice what they learned.

Including the teachings of Paul about the spiritual gifts.

An unimpeachable teacher of the Bible in Palo Alto was a man named Ray Stedman. He had started attracting Stanford University students who had lots of enthusiasm. Soon the church began a gift-shaped Sunday evening service in which they wanted the Spirit to guide what happened. They quickly discovered the power and radical democracy of spiritual gifts. If I remember it right, they felt a bit nervous about tongues. Still, Stedman wrote a book about how this revival of young Christians formed what he called *body life*. In fact, he titled his book *Body Life* (clever, eh?).

Why tell this story? Because the spiritual gifts movement we see in almost all evangelical churches today owes its origins to Ray Stedman and the body life movement at Peninsula Bible Church. When we let the Spirit take over, we lose control of what the Spirit might do—and what the Spirit might do is revive us again. The Spirit's movement among us transforms us from where we are to where God wants us to be.

Warm Up

1. In what areas of your life would you say your behavior is mostly tov? Explain.

2. In what areas of your life would you say your behavior is largely not tov? Explain.

3. In what ways is the Spirit most clearly at work in you today? Explain.

4. In what ways is the Spirit most clearly at work in your church or organization? Explain.

Get Some Insight

1. Read 2 Chronicles 19:3 and Acts 11:24. How is the word *good* used in these texts? What, if anything, does this suggest to you?

2. What gifts/workings/manifestations of the Spirit do you see in your life? How are they adding to the tov culture of your church or organization?

3. How are you getting your "radar up and ready" (see pages 181–182)? What will this mean for you?

Do the Hard Work

1. What might it mean in your church or organization to let go and let the Spirit of God go to work? Get a small group of trusted associates together to answer this question collectively. Give several specifics.

2. Spend a significant time in prayer this week, asking the Lord what *you* need to do (or stop doing) to let go and let the Spirit of God go to work. After your week of prayer, what did you learn through the Spirit?

3. Gather a small group of trusted associates and spend a significant time in prayer over the next month, asking the Lord what you *all* need to do (or stop doing) to let go and let the Spirit of God go to work. After your month of prayer, what did all of you learn through the Spirit?

11

DEPEND ON GRACE

TRANSFORMATION IS ALL FROM GOD, and we can look at God's empowering work through several terms and categories. The energies of the congregation and the Spirit of God can be summed up as well in "the grace of God."

Many are aware of the powerful motivation among young adults today to change our society. One of their major concerns is racism. The rising generation is determined to eradicate systemic racism in their generation.

Contemporary architects of social change include Stephen Charles Mott, who may be evangelicalism's most influential author on the subject. In reading his book *Biblical Ethics and Social Change* recently, I (Scot) noticed that he, too, has a deep concern with the energies needed to effect deep transformation. He devotes an entire chapter to the absolute necessity for God's grace to be at work in those who want deep social transformation.[1]

God's redeeming grace has two aspects: (1) grace is God's power *for us*, the work of pardon and justification through atonement by the Son; (2) grace is also God's power *in us*, the work of sanctification by the Spirit of God, as well as the Spirit's work in drawing us to repentance and transforming us.[2]

Genuine transformation toward tov requires the grace of God.

GETTING OVER A BAD HABIT

When we hear the word *grace*, we tend to immediately fuse it to the term *undeserved*. So much so that many times we think we must feel bad and get down-in-the-dumps depressed to experience the true meaning of grace. We need to get over it. Such a perspective reduces the meaning of grace to "God's goodness to the undeserving." Though it's true that God's grace extends to the undeserving, that phrase falls far short of telling the whole story. In a chapter about grace in my book *A Fellowship of Differents*, I try to describe the wideness and height and depth of the New Testament's message about God's grace:

Paul knew he was in a place called grace.

Grace is the opening word that tumbles out of Paul's mouth.
Grace is more than being lucky to be on God's side.
Grace is God's goodness showered on people who have failed.
Grace is God's love on those who think they are unlovable.
Grace is God knowing what we are designed to be.
Grace is God believing in us when we have given up.
Grace is someone at the end of their rope finding new
  strength.

But there's more to grace. Grace is both a *place* and a *power*.

Grace is God unleashing his transforming power.
Grace realigns and reroutes a life and a community.
Grace is when you turn your worst enemy into your
  best friend.

Grace takes people as they are and makes them what they
can be.
Grace ennobles; grace empowers.
Grace forgives; grace frees.
Grace transcends, and grace transforms. . . .
Grace turns God-fighters into God-defenders.
Grace turns Jesus-haters into Jesus-lovers.
Grace turns Spirit-resisters into Spirit-listeners.

To do this, grace forgives and grace heals and grace
transforms and grace ennobles and grace empowers. Grace
makes people in the salad bowl comfortable with one
another. Only grace can do that. *But grace can do that.*[3]

Grace in the Bible is not just the good luck we have in our redemption. No, grace is God reaching out to us in love. Grace is God touch-
ing us with redemption and forming a loving relational bond with us.
Grace is God's love prompting us to return to him with thanksgiving,
transforming us into grace agents, and then empowering us to reach
out to others to touch them with God's grace too.

In our previous book, I (Scot) quoted one of my all-time favorite
lines—from James D. G. Dunn, a New Testament scholar and one of
my teachers. He said that the Spirit at work in us *"transcends human
ability and transforms human inability."*[4]

If we are to transform our church culture (let us say this one more
time), it will not be because we are smart enough or talented enough
or shrewd enough or educated enough or systematic enough. The
deep, deep work of transforming a church culture from what it is
to what it needs to be is the work of God, who in his grace grants
us the wisdom and power to transcend our human abilities and to
transform our human inabilities into capacities we never could have
expected.

Church culture transformation is a gift of God.

And gifts are given to be received.

THE GRACE WE WILL NEED

Let's explore some of the inner workings of grace at work in churches that transform from toxic patterns of the flesh into tov patterns of the Spirit.

1. Grace is a gift.

Gifts, when given to others, form a special bond between giver and receiver, rooted in the underlying act of grace. This works in the church in two ways. First, God's gift to us of Christ and experienced by us in the Spirit creates a bond between us and God (Father, Son, and Spirit). Second, and at the same time, we become grace givers to others because of what we have received from God, forming deep social bonds with those with whom we share our gifts.

Think now of what Paul calls the Spirit's "gifts." God gives them to us and we, in turn, contribute them to others. When others accept, welcome, and embrace our contribution, they form a bond with us, and then we receive and embrace their gifts to us. That's what spiritual gifts are: gifts from God through us to others who then contribute from God through them to us.

Think of what happens when someone in your circle gives you a gift. What do you do? You not only say, "Thank you," but you immediately go into full gear wondering what you can give in return. What happens then? You become people united by gift giving. That's grace.

2. We must ask for the gift of courage to face the grace of truth and truth telling.

Too often those with power or those who sinned or those who made a bad judgment immediately appeal to the grace of forgiveness so they can stamp "Paid" on their account. Slow down! Genuine grace in a church that wants transformation from toxic patterns of the flesh to tov patterns of the Spirit will give people the courage to face the truth of their toxicity. Some stories need to be told, some words need to be admitted, and some decisions need to be undone or rectified. For healing from toxicity to occur, we will have to admit these difficult truths. Truth telling is on the path to tov.

3. We must ask for the grace to receive gifts.

When someone offers you, let's say, a gift of food or fellowship or forgiveness, you sense (because you are human) that your reception of the gift will in some sense form a bond with and an obligation to that person. Here is where many churches stumble and fall apart. Accepting the gift entails inner transformation. Churches sometimes fail to pray for God's gift of courage to face the gift giving of others in ways that can create a bond of unity and peace among us.

A pause for a reminder: This is hard work because it can bring deep pain. It can be so far beyond us that we will cry out to God: "How?" and "Why?" As James Dunn said, the Spirit at work in us transcends our ability and transforms our inability.

One time I (Scot) spoke at a church in the Pacific Northwest. Over dinner I sat next to the pastor, who began to tell me about the vision *he'd* had for his church, a vision that virtually no one else embraced. The church subsequently began a time of asking, talking, and listening to its community. They discovered that the neighborhood needed after-school care for children from homes with two working parents, or with single parents who couldn't get off work early enough. The pastor looked at me and said, "There was *no way* I was going to get involved in an after-school service."

Nevertheless, he listened, the Spirit went to work, the grace of God provided, and the next thing that happened—you guessed it—they started teaching Hebrew! No, just kidding. They worked with families in the church, with the budget committee, with local authorities, with school leaders, and together they formed an after-school ministry that served their community and transformed their church into a ministry adapted for their missional context. The Spirit gave them the courage to face it all, and the Spirit transcended and transformed.

4. We can ask God for the gift of listening to one another.

Listening to one another requires that we first talk to one another. We have all known situations where we found it very hard to listen to one another because of fear, or we flatly refused to talk to one another. Talking can break the ice . . . but listening is another matter altogether.

Listening to another person doesn't mean we agree with them. It means we pay keen attention, eyeball to eyeball (or email to email), and hear so well what the other person says that we can characterize their words so accurately that they say, "Yes, that's exactly what I said." We strike home with them. Talking and listening with another does not mean we find immediate agreement or even reach the embrace of fellowship. It simply means that we hear the other person in such a way that we truly perceive and understand what he or she says.

Beth Moore is an agent of grace to her critics (of whom she has many) on Twitter. Read this recent thread of grace, posted on her account on August 9, 2022. If you don't know about Beth and the world of social media, she receives lots of sideswipes and behind-the-back criticism. When you become as influential as she has—and a *woman* in what many see as a for-men-only world—you become vulnerable to attack. When attacked, we instinctively fight back—which she does with grace and kindness:

> This is a cheerfully written, good-will word to my beloved kin in Christ who deeply disapprove of my accepting a handful of invitations a year from pastors who graciously ask if I would speak on a Sunday to their congregations. I need you to know that I hear you.
>
> I see your deep commitment to your stand on women's roles & I admire that you never tire of the subject. I acknowledge that, at the end of your open-minded & extensive exegesis of all the NT has to say about women, you hang your hat on the verses telling women to be silent in church. I get it.

I've read them once or twice or 500X myself. I too love
the Bible. I too have studied it & value it so highly, I'll spend
my life, God willing, calling people into its pages. And after
my own extensive study of women in the NT, I hang my head
covering on verses like Acts 2:17-18, & on those where the
same Paul who wrote your final word on women references
hosts of women who were obviously colaborers in the gospel
work & among the leaders in their churches. I also burn alive
inside with the call of Christ to the great commission. . . .

All of this is to this point: if my story about Keith Moore
falling fast asleep on the front row of a church in full view
of the choir while I was bringing a message does not—at the
very least—make you grin at my expense, consider hanging
up your sheriff's badge for a few weeks and taking a vacation.

Everybody, including me, knows how you feel about
women in church. You've done your job. We get it. We hear
it. We see your commitment to the cause. But take a break.
These are sorrowful times. Have a hearty laugh on me. It's
good medicine.[5]

We don't know how you might respond to Beth Moore's words,
but we think it takes a lot of grace to be an agent of grace when you
receive as much criticism as she gets. Beth Moore listened to her critics and then responded with words of grace.

That kind of listening can lead to mutual understanding and
embracing one another, even if we continue to disagree or have vary-
ing viewpoints. (I, Scot, don't think I will ever agree with some of
my theological sparring partners, but I do believe I know what they
think.) Agreeing to disagree is a dimension of church life that can
lead beyond the disagreement to a willingness to work together on
projects.

5. We need the grace of fellowship.

We've seen this theme already at work because it is so pervasive in
church transformation. When toxic patterns emerge in a church,

fellowship breaks down, divisions form, sides are taken, and we become agents of opposition to one another. "Fellowship" in the New Testament, a translation of the Greek work *koinonia*, means sharing a common life. "Doing life together" has become a trendy expression for fellowship, but don't let its trendiness get in the way. Genuine fellowship means doing life together, which can involve dozens of actions: reading a book together, having coffee, emailing prayers for one another, sharing something sad or glad in a way that promotes grieving with someone or rejoicing in their joy.

6. We need the grace of mutual gift reception.

Let's say that in the toxic atmosphere you've experienced, someone else got to sing on the worship team and you didn't. Or they got chosen to lead a committee or a team or an event. Or they were plat-formed for a speaking event and you weren't. Some bitterness, resent-ment, ill will, and gossipy words intentionally were set loose into some circles in the church, where they have festered for some time.

When tov becomes the church's cultural vision, some of these toxins of resentment will have to be dealt with. God will work to transform you into a person who accepts another person's oppor-tunities and strives toward rejoicing over that person's gifts (if even with the occasional *ugh* and *argh*). This requires truth telling, grace, forgiveness, grace, acceptance, and more grace.

7. We need grace to face the reality of a toxic culture that must be transformed.

This requires getting on board with whatever direction the journey toward tov is taking. Let's say your church has slumbered into a pas-sive we're-a-Sunday-only kind of church. Let's say your church wakes up to critical needs in your community, whether evangelism, jus-tice, or physical support. Your church leadership, employing clear communication among the congregation, forms a mission strategy to become locally present in a way that can only be called a congrega-tional response to local needs. Let's say you're not especially gung ho about this. Go ahead, admit it. Or let's say you are totally gung ho and your closest friend in the church clearly is not. In these situations, we need grace to face the new direction, the change, the transformation, as something God can do—even if you're not quite ready to say this new direction is "something God *is doing*." People like us will need grace for this kind of transformation to occur.

8. We need grace for others.

One pastor often tells his church that the problem with grace is not with grace, but with us. That is, we don't really *like* grace—at least, not for others. For them, we want judgment. For us, we *love* grace. No doubt, toxic cultures have plenty to judge. But behind every behavior lies a story, and every story cries out for grace. As you transform a toxic culture toward tov, don't lose sight of giving grace, or you may find *yourself* being the toxic one.

GRACE IS MORE

Just before bringing this to an end, let's back up and remind ourselves that grace includes, but is much more than, "You don't deserve the gift." Grace is the loving action of our totally tov God to reach out to us in love, to shower us with gifts of redemption, so we can be transformed into the image of God in Christ through the power of the indwelling Spirit. For that transformation to occur, especially in churches mired in toxins, we will need multiple graces of social bonding, truth telling, talking and listening to one another, fellowship, the mutuality of gift reception, and getting on board as the church moves into a tov-er culture.

Most churches trying to work toward tov discover that the Spirit often works on a timeline much slower or more nuanced than theirs. Only with time and in hindsight can they typically see what the Spirit has been up to.

Consider, for example, Beaverton Christian Church (BCC) in Oregon. In 2016, after ninety years of existence and having reached a peak attendance of 2,500, the congregation faced the harsh reality of seeing their weekly numbers dip to less than one-seventh of former levels. They also began to realize they had drifted into some toxicity.

Meanwhile, twenty minutes away in the town of West Linn, Willamette Christian Church (WCC), out of their desire to see Kingdom growth in the greater Portland area, had been praying for months about where God might have them plant another campus. They had looked at more than forty properties, but God had not opened a single door.

One day, the leaders of BCC invited the leadership team at WCC to coach them on how to become more tov. By then, the Beaverton church had lost their lead pastor but still earnestly desired to serve their community well. The church's elders soon committed themselves to a new relationship with WCC, and in time, WCC adopted BCC, though both churches kept their respective names to better represent and reach their local communities.

"It was never about bigger numbers or bigger buildings," said Grant Hickman, executive pastor of coaching at WCC, "but always about how the Spirit was moving in grace to magnify Jesus."

As both churches performed their due diligence and looked into their histories, they discovered that God had been at work *long* before either congregation or staff became aware of the other. It turned out that, sixty years earlier, BCC had begun praying about planting a church near West Linn, which at the time had only about three thousand residents. Not long afterward, the leaders of BCC and other affiliated churches in the area came together to plant, underwrite, and support the planting of a new congregation named . . . Willamette Christian Church.[6]

Only God the Holy Spirit could work so graciously and on such an extended timeline. One church planted another, and more than half a century later, the planted church helped the original church improve its soil and thus move into its next generation of fruitful ministry. Today, both BCC and WCC have flourishing, tov-flavored ministries designed to help their local communities see and experience the grace of the Lord Jesus Christ.

Before you go any further forward in the good work of church transformation, spend some time pondering that it is not about *you* doing the work, no matter how hard you have been co-laboring with God. It is God, God's Spirit, and the sheer grace of God that empowers you to collaborate with God toward tov. Let us remember Paul's words to the church in Corinth:

> By the grace of God I am what I am, and his grace to me was not without effect. No, I worked harder than all of them— yet not I, but the grace of God that was with me.
>
> 1 CORINTHIANS 15:10

Do you want to see transformation, experience tov, and find joy? Only by depending on God's grace can you and I get every bit of that.

Warm Up

1. Ask three people who know you well to identify where they have seen God's grace most evident in your life, working to transform you into a more tov person.

2. Get together with a few close associates to discuss where you have seen God's grace most at work in your church or organization, transforming it into something more tov.

3. Discuss with a few close associates where you most need to see God's grace at work in your church or organization to transform it into something more tov.

Get Some Insight

1. Approach several safe people in your church or organization and ask each of them two brief questions:

   a. Where do you see God's grace most at work in our church or organization?
   b. Where do you least see God's grace at work in our church or organization?

2. Gather a few close associates at your church or organization and discuss two brief questions:

   a. Where do we most desire to see God's grace transcend our human abilities in this place?
   b. Where do we most desire to see God's grace transform our human inabilities in this place?

Do the Hard Work

In a safe group of associates and peers, ask the following questions about your church or organization:

1. What deep social bonds are forming here because of God's grace? Where are they *not* forming where they need to? Why aren't they?

2. What kind of courage do we need as a group to face the grace of truth telling? What truth are we most afraid to hear?

3. Take some time to pray for the grace of gift reception. What kind of pain might you have to endure when God answers this prayer?

4. Ask God for the gift of listening to one another. Ask him especially to reveal to you those individuals or groups to whom you have not been listening.

5. In what ways does your church or organization do a pretty good job of "doing life together"? In what ways does it *not* do a good job here? Explain.

6. How does your church or organization most need to get better in the grace of *mutual* gift reception? Explain. How does this grace differ from the grace of gift reception (as in question 3 above)?

7. What is the hardest reality you face regarding a toxic culture in your church or organization? What kind of grace do you need to face this reality? Name it.

TOV IS
WORTH IT

THERE IS NO SUCH THING as a perfect church. But there are healthy churches, unwell churches, toxic churches, and dead churches. However, when you choose to do the hard work of upgrading your church's soil and eagerly partner with God to grow healthy fruit, you will experience for yourself the joys of a tov church. The pivot is worth it, even if you get dizzy in the spin.

We offer you now an exhortation for the challenge you have chosen to accept—namely, culture transformation in your church.

First, we encourage you to make character formation, both for individuals and the church as a culture, the most important mission of your local church. There are a number of ways to express this kind of character—we like the term *tov* as a comprehensive mission term—but it is wise to keep a number of terms and biblical themes in view. We need the law of Moses, the prophets, Jesus and the Sermon on the Mount, Paul's vision of life in the Spirit, John's emphasis on love, and Revelation's vision of faithful allegiance. Whichever terms come up as you move forward, keep *character* first and foremost.

Second, be patient. A vision is a wonderful thing until you meet the first bloc of resistance (and the second and the third). One step at a time may be the most important idea, along with the proper use of power. Patient transformation agents will need to become expert listeners and constant adjusters. The idea that a vision can be hatched in one person's study—a vision that everyone will embrace with enthusiasm—didn't happen with Jesus, with Paul, or with Peter. It didn't happen with Luther or Wesley. It didn't happen with W. E. B. Du Bois or Martin Luther King Jr. To form a genuine coalition requires patient vision-casting and constant conversation, from which everyone learns and grows.

Third, an important word to acknowledge in church transformation is *pain*. Yes, that's the right word. Just ask any transforming congregation. In this book we have emphasized Oak Hills Church in California (which pursued a spiritual formation model) and New Hope Church in Oregon (which pursued a pared-down focus on following Jesus). The experience of pastoring these churches through transformation has been exhausting and even agonizing at times. But if you ask John and Corrie Rosensteel of New Hope, they will tell you that as they pondered all the changes in their lives over the last decade, they came to realize that their church is healthier and more like Jesus than it had been in a long time.

> Tears welled in our eyes as we sat silently with that realization. It was a bittersweet moment. The last six years have taken a heavy toll. Yet when we step back to see what God has done, and hopefully what God still intends to do, we are grateful. Our path has been populated with Ebenezer stones [reminders of God's help in times of need]. We continue to pray that New Hope would continue to become the church God has created us to be. And we regularly remind ourselves of a truth our church and family rallies around—all is grace.[1]

Church transformation is painful. It is bittersweet. Yet it is *worth it*.

Fourth, it takes courage. Some of your best friends and biggest supporters will turn on you or at least turn away from the transformation plans. Pastor after pastor told us the same story. Take courage in God's work, in the grace of God, and in the power of the Spirit to bring change. Avoid all temptations to coerce others and instead walk in the will of God and let God do the work.

Finally, expect surprises! Here's one from New Hope that John Rosensteel never anticipated when he first entered the front door to begin his ministry there:

We were able to pay our mortgage but felt our megachurch building did not position us well for the type of church God was calling us to become. Unexpectedly, a large Vietnamese Catholic church that was limited by their facility bought our building. It felt like a miracle. We were able to pay off our debt and walk away with a surplus to invest in a new space more fitting to our mission. We were without a suitable meeting space for a while as we waited for God to move. Then, out of nowhere, a nearby church reached out and wondered whether we might want to adopt them. It felt like another miracle. They fully owned a beautiful building nestled on prime acreage in Southeast Portland. It was a perfect fit. We completed the adoption and had our first in-person gathering as one church in our new home after the COVID lockdown ended.

How sweet is that? God has been extremely generous to us. All is grace. We are presently prayerfully exploring opportunities to join with other Portland area churches in new Kingdom endeavors. We never would have been in a place to consider these possibilities if we had stayed put and played it safe. When we began to focus more on who we were *becoming* than on where we were going, we were able to confidently entrust our next steps to God. And God provided for us in ways that exceeded our wildest hopes and imaginations. As we continue to seek to become a tov church, we can't wait to discover what God has in store for us around the bend. I'm guessing it will be unexpected. I know it will be good.[2]

Here's a watchword for the patient, courageous work of pursuing character formation in a church: *You have no idea* what God might do through your church in your community. Planning is a great idea . . . until God introduces a turn and a transformation.

Be ready to pivot.

ACKNOWLEDGMENTS

SCOT

Thank you to Jon Farrar and Jan Long Harris at Tyndale House.

Thank you to Steve Halliday for enthusiastically entering into this family project, and for your advice on the (re)arrangement of chapters.

To the men and women who trusted us with their stories, many of whom were wounded in the process of their resistance: We hold your words sacredly and pray that this book honors your courage, your hope, your advocacy for a better way forward. This book is for all who long for tov transformation.

LAURA

While writing this book about culture transformation, I realized I was in the midst of my own transformation story. I found myself living what I was writing—entering into God's work while he transformed me. I am changed by his kindness and grace.

I wish to mention my gratitude for several people in particular: Kelsey, Cari, Amanda, Jaime, and Ruth; as well as Brooke and Chris. I am deeply thankful for the tov examples in my own life. Nader and Karin and Tom, *thank you* does not cover all that I wish to express. I can only say how very blessed I am to have such examples of goodness in my life, as well as friends who show up at my door or call spontaneously; for others who hopped a plane without hesitation or invited us into their homes and lives every Wednesday evening.

And mostly to Mark. I love you. How thankful I am for the deep beauty of God's transformative work. He makes all things new.

THE TOV TOOL

THIS SURVEY CAN BE TAKEN in its entirety or by section, but it is designed to generate both knowledge about a church and even more conversation among people who are safe with one another. Wise people will know how to use questions like these. But for you to discern your culture and learn, you will need to ask questions in a safe context. Make sure the candid answers of concerned people do not become a source of recrimination.

This is not a normed survey, nor has it been validated by social scientists. But we pray it will help you discern your culture and create candid conversation points about your church's overall health.

When X is used in a question, it represents your church or institution.

EMPATHY

Empathy is the capacity to understand other people in their pain or joy, to enter into their pain or joy, and to experience it with them as an act of love and for the purpose of caring for them well.

> 1. Is X characterized by empathy, especially for the vulnerable?
>
> Always–Often–Rarely–Never–Don't know
>
> 2. Are women treated with empathy?
>
> Always–Often–Rarely–Never–Don't know

3. Are persons of color treated with empathy?

Always–Often–Rarely–Never–Don't know

4. Are persons from other cultures and ethnicities treated with empathy?

Always–Often–Rarely–Never–Don't know

5. Are persons with less education treated with empathy?

Always–Often–Rarely–Never–Don't know

6. Are persons of less income treated with empathy?

Always–Often–Rarely–Never–Don't know

7. Are persons of less skill treated with empathy?

Always–Often–Rarely–Never–Don't know

8. Do you listen to such persons in order to expand your inclusiveness?

Always–Often–Rarely–Never–Don't know

9. Do such persons say they are listened to?

Always–Often–Rarely–Never–Don't know

10. Is X characterized by self-centeredness and a lack of empathy for others?

Always–Often–Rarely–Never–Don't know

11. When people are let go or fired or they resign, is their memory erased and are they demeaned in a routine manner by those above you or around you? Is there now a customary negative narrative about such people?

Always–Often–Rarely–Never–Don't know

GRACE

Tov churches have a character trait of grace, which is all about a gift given and a relationship established. For the receiver of the gift, these factors elicit both gratitude and gift-giving back to the giver, and they also form the receiver into an agent of grace.

1. Is X characterized by grace toward those who are beginning in their Christlikeness and giftedness?

   Always–Often–Rarely–Never–Don't know

2. Is X characterized by grace toward those who are struggling?

   Always–Often–Rarely–Never–Don't know

3. Is X characterized by grace toward those who fail?

   Always–Often–Rarely–Never–Don't know

4. Are some given more grace than others?

   Always–Often–Rarely–Never–Don't know

5. Is God's grace for us prominent in our relationships with one another?

   Always–Often–Rarely–Never–Don't know

6. Are we treated first as siblings in Christ?

   Always–Often–Rarely–Never–Don't know

7. Is God's grace making those above you and around you aware of their dependence on God?

   Always–Often–Rarely–Never–Don't know

8. Is God's grace shaping others into expressions of forgiveness?

   Always–Often–Rarely–Never–Don't know

9. Is God's grace empowering those above you and around you to transcend their natural skills?

Always—Often—Rarely—Never—Don't know

10. Is God's grace trusted enough to permit persons to grow in Christ and in their gifts and skills?

Always—Often—Rarely—Never—Don't know

11. Is X characterized by people fearing their pastor, their associates, their directors, other staff, or congregants?

Always—Often—Rarely—Never—Don't know

12. Do you fear your pastor, the associates, the directors, staff, or congregants?

Always—Often—Rarely—Never—Don't know

13. Is X characterized by people who fear for their job or status if they ask questions or speak up?

Always—Often—Rarely—Never—Don't know

14. Do you fear for your job in the church or status if you were to ask questions or speak up?

Always—Often—Rarely—Never—Don't know

15. Is X characterized by people who adjust their behaviors and even appearance based on what others say or might say or have said?

Always—Often—Rarely—Never—Don't know

16. Do you adjust your behaviors or appearance based on what others say, might say, or have said?

Always—Often—Rarely—Never—Don't know

PEOPLE FIRST

Tov churches are known for putting people first.

1. Is X characterized by a people-first culture?

   Always–Often–Rarely–Never–Don't know

2. Are you known as a people-first person?

   Always–Often–Rarely–Never–Don't know

3. Do those above you and around you in hierarchy know your name, your family members, your story?

   Always–Often–Rarely–Never–Don't know

4. Do you know the names and families and stories of those above and around you?

   Always–Often–Rarely–Never–Don't know

5. Is X characterized by an institution-first culture?

   Always–Often–Rarely–Never–Don't know

6. Is the institution constantly the center of discussion?

   Always–Often–Rarely–Never–Don't know

7. Are people affirmed for their gifts and contributions?

   Always–Often–Rarely–Never–Don't know

8. Are your own ideas, hopes, suggestions, and innovations rejected before consideration?

   Always–Often–Rarely–Never–Don't know

9. Do you at times feel lost in the system and the vision and the mission?

Always–Often–Rarely–Never–Don't know

10. Does X adjust well to new people?

Always–Often–Rarely–Never–Don't know

11. Does your group sometimes hope some in the group would just leave or resign?

Always–Often–Rarely–Never–Don't know

12. How often has your group adjusted so that your gifts are appreciated?

Always–Often–Rarely–Never–Don't know

13. Were you consulted, if appropriate, for the formation of the vision and mission of X?

Always–Often–Rarely–Never–Don't know

TRUTH

Tov churches are known for a commitment to truth.

1. Is X characterized by people who live in the reality of truth?

Always–Often–Rarely–Never–Don't know

2. Is X a safe place for you?

Always–Often–Rarely–Never–Don't know

3. Is it safe for you to talk about safety?

Always–Often–Rarely–Never–Don't know

4. Is there a gracious humility to confront the truth about X
   and yourself?

   Always–Often–Rarely–Never–Don't know

5. Is dissent permissible?

   Always–Often–Rarely–Never–Don't know

6. Is X characterized by people who ignore truth, even
   though its reality is known and knowable to some
   extent?

   Always–Often–Rarely–Never–Don't know

7. Is X characterized by people who spin the reality?

   Always–Often–Rarely–Never–Don't know

8. Is X characterized by people who falsify the reality?

   Always–Often–Rarely–Never–Don't know

9. Is X characterized by people who deny the reality?

   Always–Often–Rarely–Never–Don't know

10. Is X characterized by people who suppress the reality?

    Always–Often–Rarely–Never–Don't know

11. Is X characterized by people who suppress those speaking
    up about the reality?

    Always–Often–Rarely–Never–Don't know

12. Is X characterized by people who are associated with
    whistleblowers?

    Always–Often–Rarely–Never–Don't know

JUSTICE

Tov churches are known for a commitment to justice.

1. Is X characterized by people who do the right thing and act justly in the sense that they do what conforms to Christlikeness?

   Always–Often–Rarely–Never–Don't know

2. Does X spell out what the "right thing" means in appropriate situations?

   Always–Often–Rarely–Never–Don't know

3. Is the right thing done by those above you and around you?

   Always–Often–Rarely–Never–Don't know

4. Is the "right thing" fudged so it appears to be the right thing when people know it is not?

   Always–Often–Rarely–Never–Don't know

5. Is the "right thing" seemingly assumed but never expressed?

   Always–Often–Rarely–Never–Don't know

6. Does the "right thing," though never clearly articulated, become suddenly stated and then used for rebukes or demotions or firings?

   Always–Often–Rarely–Never–Don't know

7. Is the wrong thing sometimes done but hidden so others think the right thing is being done?

   Always–Often–Rarely–Never–Don't know

8. Is X characterized by people for whom loyalty transcends the right thing?

Always–Often–Rarely–Never–Don't know

9. Are you ever asked to do what you think is wrong because it will benefit X or the system?

Always–Often–Rarely–Never–Don't know

10. Have you ever asked someone to do what may be wrong because it will benefit X or the system?

Always–Often–Rarely–Never–Don't know

SERVICE

Tov churches are known for prioritizing service to others.

1. Is your pastor a celebrity?

Always–Often–Rarely–Never–Don't know

2. Is your pastor treated like a celebrity or star?

Always–Often–Rarely–Never–Don't know

3. Is X characterized by people who serve others?

Always–Often–Rarely–Never–Don't know

4. Do you think you are being served as you should be in a Christlike culture?

Always–Often–Rarely–Never–Don't know

5. Do people at X serve others in a way that at least some do not always know about those acts of service?

Always–Often–Rarely–Never–Don't know

6. Does X think serving others is the way of Christ?

Always–Often–Rarely–Never–Don't know

7. Are you all "serve" and never "being served"?

Always–Often–Rarely–Never–Don't know

8. Is X characterized by people above you and around you who expect to be served?

Always–Often–Rarely–Never–Don't know

9. Is X characterized by persons who resent serving others?

Always–Often–Rarely–Never–Don't know

10. Is X characterized by persons who demand to be served?

Always–Often–Rarely–Never–Don't know

11. Is X characterized by persons who are angered if they are not being served by others?

Always–Often–Rarely–Never–Don't know

12. Is service expected or demanded in ways that degrade or shame or are inappropriate?

Always–Often–Rarely–Never–Don't know

NOTES

FOREWORD

1. Mike Tyson, "Mike Tyson on His Iconic Saying 'Everyone Got a Plan Until They're Punched in the Face,'" EsNews, YouTube video, 0:54, October 2, 2021, https://www.youtube.com/watch?v=MEtFk9KaglA.
2. Paul Batalden, quoted in Leslie Proctor, "Editor's Notebook: A Quotation with a Life of Its Own," *Patient Safety & Quality Healthcare* (blog), July 1, 2008, https://www.psqh.com/analysis/editor-s-notebook-a-quotation-with-a-life-of-its-own/.
3. J. R. R. Tolkien, *The Return of the King: Being the Third Part of the Lord of the Rings* (New York: Quality Paperback Book Club, 2001), 230.

INTRODUCTION: UNTIL CHRIST IS FORMED IN US

1. Edgar H. Schein, *Organizational Culture and Leadership*, 4th ed. (San Francisco: Jossey-Bass, 2010), 29. Schein brilliantly describes culture using the image of a lily pond. In this book we adapt that idea to a peach tree.

CHAPTER 1: TRANSFORMATION IS POSSIBLE, BUT NOT EASY

1. Kent Carlson and Mike Lueken, *Renovation of the Church: What Happens When a Seeker Church Discovers Spiritual Formation* (Downers Grove, IL: IVP Books, 2011), 20.
2. Carlson and Lueken, 20.
3. Carlson and Lueken, 23.
4. Carlson and Lueken, 25.
5. Carlson and Lueken, 27–28.
6. Carlson and Lueken, 32, 35. Italics added.
7. Carlson and Lueken, 41.
8. Carlson and Lueken, 115.
9. Carlson and Lueken, 135. Italics added.
10. Carlson and Lueken, 135.
11. Carlson and Lueken, 136–137.
12. Carlson and Lueken, 177.

13. These points are my (Scot's) versions of themes discussed in Benedetta Craveri, *The Age of Conversation*, trans. Teresa Waugh (New York: NYRB, 2005).

CHAPTER 2: CHANGE STARTS WITH THE SOIL

1. Chuck DeGroat, "Narcissistic Leadership in the Church," *Catalyst* (online newsletter), October 13, 2021, catalystresources.org/narcissistic-leadership-in -the-church. See also Chuck DeGroat, *When Narcissism Comes to Church: Healing Your Community from Emotional and Spiritual Abuse* (Downers Grove, IL: IVP, 2020), and Craig Williford and Carolyn Williford, *How to Treat a Staff Infection: Resolving Problems in Your Church or Ministry Team* (Grand Rapids, MI: Baker Books, 2008).
2. Adapted from Dr. Paul White, "Can a Christian Business Be a Toxic Workplace?" *Faith Driven Entrepreneur*, accessed October 26, 2022, https://www.faithdriven entrepreneur.org/blog/can-a-christian-business-be-a-toxic-workplace.
3. Anne-Marie Slaughter, *Renewal: From Crisis to Transformation in Our Lives, Work, and Politics* (Princeton, NJ: Princeton University Press, 2021), 19.
4. Slaughter, 92. Italics in the original.
5. Edgar H. Schein, *Organizational Culture and Leadership*, 4th ed. (San Francisco: Jossey-Bass, 2010), 28–29.
6. John Rosensteel, personal account of the transformation of New Hope Church, Portland, Oregon. John wrote out the story of New Hope Church for us, and we quote from this account at various points in the book.

CHAPTER 3: FORM TOV CHARACTER

1. Noah Webster, "On the Necessity of Fostering American Identity after Independence" (1783), https://americainclass.org/sources/makingrevolution/independence/text3 /websteramericanidentity.pdf. Italics in the original.
2. Andrew Van Dam and Alyssa Fowers, "Which Birds Are the Biggest Jerks at the Feeder? A Massive Data Analysis Reveals the Answer," *Washington Post*, November 28, 2021, https://www.washingtonpost.com/business/2021/11/28/bird -feeder-pecking-order/. I (Scot) am grateful to Jonathan Hurshman for pointing me to this wonderful article.
3. These ideas are adapted from Bill Thrall, Bruce McNicol, and Ken McElrath, *The Ascent of a Leader: How Ordinary Relationships Develop Extraordinary Character and Influence* (San Francisco: Jossey-Bass, 1994).
4. Aristotle, quoted in James Q. Wilson, *On Character: Essays* (Washington, DC: AEI Press, 1995), 108.
5. Wilson, *On Character*, 108.
6. For more on this topic, see Nikki Coffey Tousley and Brad J. Kallenberg, "Virtue Ethics," in *Dictionary of Scripture and Ethics*, ed. Joel B. Green (Grand Rapids, MI: Baker Academic, 2011), 814–819; D. Michael Cox and Brad J. Kallenberg, "Character," in *Dictionary of Scripture and Ethics*, ed. Joel B. Green (Grand Rapids, MI: Baker Academic, 2011), 127–130.
7. Cox and Kallenberg, "Character," 127.
8. Cox and Kallenberg, "Character.

9. Cox and Kallenberg, "Character," 128–129.
10. Two other good strengths evaluation tools are the Gallup CliftonStrengths Assessment (https://www.gallup.com/cliftonstrengths/en/home.aspx) and Marvin Oxenham's Virtue Education (https://virtueducation.net/).
11. Christopher Peterson and Martin E. Seligman, *Character Strengths and Virtues: A Handbook and Classification* (Oxford: Oxford University Press, 2004), 13.
12. NRSV, italics added.
13. After reading an early draft of our manuscript, Greg Mamula (one of Scot's former students) suggested that we emphasize developing these virtues with others in community. We are grateful for his insight. One of Greg's books, *Table Life: An Invitation to Everyday Discipleship* (Valley Forge, PA.: Judson Press, 2020), provides a good entry into such a community life.
14. Romans 3:10.
15. Desmond Tutu and Mpho Tutu, *Made for Goodness: And Why This Makes All the Difference* (New York: HarperOne, 2011). See especially pages 1–18.
16. See, for example, James Bryan Smith, *The Good and Beautiful God: Falling in Love with the God Jesus Knows* (Downers Grove, IL: IVP Books, 2009); James Bryan Smith, *The Good and Beautiful Life: Putting on the Character of Christ* (Downers Grove, IL: IVP Books, 2010); James Bryan Smith, *The Good and Beautiful Community: Following the Spirit, Extending Grace, Demonstrating Love* (Downers Grove, IL: IVP Books, 2010); Barry D. Jones, *Dwell: Life with God for the World* (Downers Grove, IL: IVP Books, 2014); David E. Fitch, *Faithful Presence: Seven Disciplines That Shape the Church for Mission* (Downers Grove, IL: IVP, 2017).
17. Zach W. Lambert (@ZachWLambert), October 22, 2021, https://mobile.twitter.com/ZachWLambert/status/1451559642992201737.
18. Zach W. Lambert (@ZachWLambert), October 22, 2021.
19. Martha C. Nussbaum, *Citadels of Pride: Sexual Assault, Accountability, and Reconciliation* (New York: W. W. Norton, 2021), 151.
20. Tiffany Bluhm, *Prey Tell: Why We Silence Women Who Tell the Truth and How Everyone Can Speak Up* (Grand Rapids, MI: Brazos, 2021), 100.
21. Bluhm, *Prey Tell*, 107.
22. Private correspondence with Scot McKnight, July 27, 2001.
23. Jennifer J. Freyd, "What Is a Betrayal Trauma? What Is Betrayal Trauma Theory?" accessed October 27, 2022, https://dynamic.uoregon.edu/jjf/defineBT.html. See also Jennifer Freyd and Pamela Birrell, *Blind to Betrayal: Why We Fool Ourselves We Aren't Being Fooled* (Hoboken, NJ: Wiley, 2013). The concept of betrayal abuse was brought to our attention through Lori Anne Thompson, a survivor of abuse by Ravi Zacharias. See Lori Anne Thompson, "Clergy Sexual Abuse as a Betrayal Trauma: Institutional Betrayal & A Call for Courageous Response," Lori Anne Thompson blog, September 18, 2020, https://loriannethompson.com/2020/09/18/clergy-sexual-abuse-as-a-betrayal-trauma-institutional-betrayal-a-call-for-courageous-response/.
24. James Ullrich, "Corporate Stockholm Syndrome," *Psychology Today*, March 14, 2014, https://www.psychologytoday.com/us/blog/the-modern-time-crunch/201403/corporate-stockholm-syndrome.

CHAPTER 4: PRACTICE TOV POWER

1. We have learned much from Diane Langberg, *Redeeming Power: Understanding Authority and Abuse in the Church* (Grand Rapids, MI.: Brazos, 2020), 3–17.

2. *Merriam-Webster.com Dictionary*, s.v. "power," https://www.merriam-webster.com/dictionary/power.

3. Lisa Oakley and Justin Humphreys, *Escaping the Maze of Spiritual Abuse: Creating Healthy Christian Cultures* (London: SPCK, 2019), 31.

4. I (Scot) am grateful to my friend Mindy Caliguire for pointing me to Hagberg's work.

5. The phrase "The Kingdom of God . . . is a neighborhood" is from Shea Tuttle, *Exactly as You Are: The Life and Faith of Mister Rogers* (Grand Rapids, MI: Eerdmans, 2019), 109.

6. See Chris Buczinsky, "The Performance of the Pastoral," in *Revisiting Mister Rogers' Neighborhood: Essays on Lessons about Self and Community*, eds. Kathy Merlock Jackson and Steven M. Emmanuel (Jefferson, NC: McFarland and Company, 2016), 10.

7. In what follows, we summarize Martha C. Nussbaum, *Citadels of Pride: Sexual Assault, Accountability, and Reconciliation* (New York: W. W. Norton, 2021), 12–13.

8. Langberg, *Redeeming Power*, 12.

9. Hans-Ruedi Weber, *Power: Focus for a Biblical Theology* (Geneva: WCC Publications, 1989), 167.

10. Anne-Marie Slaughter, *Renewal: From Crisis to Transformation in Our Lives, Work, and Politics* (Princeton, NJ: Princeton University Press, 2021), 81.

11. *Mr. Rogers' Neighborhood*, episode 1466, air date February 4, 1980.

12. *Mr. Rogers' Neighborhood*, episode 1362, air date April 9, 1974.

13. "Lady Aberlin and Daniel Tiger Talk and Sing about Mistakes," *Mister Rogers' Neighborhood*, season 15, episode 78, August 27, 2009.

14. *Mr. Rogers' Neighborhood*, episode 1553, air date November 27, 1985.

15. Gary Chapman, Paul White, and Harold Myra, *Rising Above a Toxic Workplace: Taking Care of Yourself in an Unhealthy Environment*, rev. ed. (Chicago: Northfield, 2014), 124. Italics in the original.

16. Tuttle, *Exactly as You Are*, 133.

17. Philip P. Hallie, *Lest Innocent Blood Be Shed: The Story of the Village of Le Chambon and How Goodness Happened There* (New York: Harper Perennial, 1994), 7.

18. Hallie, 10.

19. Hallie, 48.

20. Richard J. Foster, *The Challenge of the Disciplined Life: Christian Reflections on Money, Sex, and Power* (San Francisco: HarperSanFrancisco, 1985), 201–211.

21. Edgar H. Schein, *Organizational Culture and Leadership*, 4th ed. (San Francisco: Jossey-Bass, 2010), 158.

22. Janet O. Hagberg, *Real Power: Stages of Personal Power in Organizations*, 3rd ed. (Salem, WI: Sheffield, 2002), 200–205.

23. Julie Battilana and Tiziana Casciaro, "Don't Let Power Corrupt You," *Harvard Business Review* 99, no. 5 (September–October 2021), https://hbr.org/2021/09/dont-let-power-corrupt-you. Italics in the original.

24. Battilana and Casciaro, "Don't Let Power Corrupt You."
25. Battilana and Casciaro, "Don't Let Power Corrupt You."

CHAPTER 5: BECOME A TOV EXAMPLE

1. This section is adapted from Scot McKnight, *Pastor Paul: Nurturing a Culture of Christoformity in the Church* (Grand Rapids, MI: Brazos, 2019), 11–15.
2. Sondra Wheeler, *The Minister as Moral Theologian: Ethical Dimensions of Pastoral Leadership* (Grand Rapids, MI: Baker Academic, 2017), xiii–xiv.
3. Victor A. Copan, *Saint Paul as Spiritual Director: An Analysis of the Concept of the Imitation of Paul with Implications and Applications to the Practice of Spiritual Direction*, reprint ed., Paternoster Biblical Monographs (Eugene, OR: Wipf & Stock, 2008), 2. Italics in the original.
4. Dave Ferguson, "7 Steps to Creating a Culture That Makes Heroes," Global Leadership Network blog, April 9, 2018, https://globalleadership.org/articles /leading-organizations/7-steps-to-creating-a-culture-that-makes-heroes-dave -ferguson/. Italics in the original.
5. Peter L. Berger and Thomas Luckmann, *The Social Construction of Reality: A Treatise in the Sociology of Knowledge* (New York: Anchor, 1967), 120–121.
6. Our friend Steve Carter said something to this effect.
7. John Rosensteel, personal account of the transformation of New Hope Church, Portland, Oregon.
8. John Rosensteel, personal account.
9. Dietrich Bonhoeffer, *Letters and Papers from Prison*, ed. John W. de Gruchy (Minneapolis: Fortress, 2010), 504. Italics added.
10. Dietrich Bonhoeffer, *Theological Education at Finkenwalde: 1935–1937*, ed. H. Gaylon Barker and Mark S. Brocker, trans. Douglas W. Stott (Minneapolis: Fortress, 2013), 442. Italics added.
11. Rachel Chang, "20 Years Later: The Little Town in Newfoundland That Welcomed Nearly 7,000 Strangers on 9/11," *Travel and Leisure*, September 11, 2021, https:// www.travelandleisure.com/travel-news/newfoundland-labrador-9-11 -anniversary.
12. Chang, "20 Years Later."
13. Chang, "20 Years Later."
14. Nicholas Mercer, "Gander Looking at Options for Displaying 9/11 Steel More Prominently," SaltWire Network, August 20, 2019, https://www.saltwire.com /newfoundland-labrador/news/gander-looking-at-options-for-displaying-911 -steel-more-prominently-343064/.
15. Shea Tuttle, *Exactly as You Are: The Life and Faith of Mister Rogers* (Grand Rapids, MI: Eerdmans, 2019), 163–164.
16. Renée Roden, "His Parish Was the Poor: The Rev. Tom Lumpkin Spent 40 Years Ministering to Detroit's Homeless," Religion News Service, August 4, 2021, https:// religionnews.com/2021/08/04/his-parish-was-the-poor-fr-tom-lumpkin-spent -40-years-ministering-to-detroits-homeless/.
17. Roden, "His Parish Was the Poor."
18. Roden, "His Parish Was the Poor."

CHAPTER 6: BUILD A COALITION

1. See Kirsten Powers, *Saving Grace: Speak Your Truth, Stay Centered, and Learn to Coexist with People Who Drive You Nuts* (New York: Convergent, 2021). I (Scot) have reviewed her book in two places: https://scotmcknight.substack .com/p/under-the-gaze-of-grace, and https://religionnews.com/2021/11/09 /a-controversial-take-proposing-grace-has-a-place-in-todays-toxic-discourse/.

2. Alan Ashworth, "Head Pastor at The Chapel Is Forced Out amid Concerns over Leadership, Treatment of Staff," *Akron Beacon Journal*, August 7, 2021, https:// www.beaconjournal.com/story/news/2021/08/07/senior-pastor-chapel-resigns -akron-green-tim-armstrong-mike-castelli/5496357001/.

3. Kent Carlson and Mike Lueken, *Renovation of the Church: What Happens When a Seeker Church Discovers Spiritual Formation* (Downers Grove, IL: IVP Books, 2011), 53.

4. Edgar H. Schein, *Organizational Culture and Leadership*, 4th ed. (San Francisco: Jossey-Bass, 2010), 167.

5. Hemant Kakkar and Niro Sivanathan, "The Impact of Leader Dominance on Employees' Zero-Sum Mindset and Helping Behavior," *Journal of Applied Psychology*, 107(10), 1706–1724.

6. Nannerl Keohane, *Thinking about Leadership* (Princeton, NJ: Princeton University Press, 2012), 23.

7. Anne-Marie Slaughter, *Renewal: From Crisis to Transformation in Our Lives, Work, and Politics* (Princeton, NJ: Princeton University Press, 2021), 65–67.

8. Slaughter, *Renewal*, 67.

9. Slaughter, *Renewal*, 74.

10. John Rosensteel, personal account of the transformation of New Hope Church, Portland, Oregon.

11. Rosensteel, personal account. Italics added.

12. Rosensteel, personal account.

13. Rosensteel, personal account.

CHAPTER 7: TAKE ONE STEP AT A TIME

1. Kent Carlson and Mike Lueken, *Renovation of the Church: What Happens When a Seeker Church Discovers Spiritual Formation* (Downers Grove, IL: IVP Books, 2011), 127–128.

2. Carlson and Lueken, 16.

3. Rosensteel, personal account.

4. John Rosensteel, email to Scot McKnight, July 28, 2021. Used with permission.

5. John Rosensteel email.

CHAPTER 8: CREATE POCKETS OF TOV

1. Dietrich Bonhoeffer, *Life Together and Prayerbook of the Bible*, ed. Geffrey B. Kelly, trans. Daniel W. Bloesch and James H. Burtness (Minneapolis: Fortress, 1996), 34. See also 27–47.

2. Kent Carlson and Mike Lueken, *Renovation of the Church: What Happens When a Seeker Church Discovers Spiritual Formation* (Downers Grove, IL: IVP Books, 2011), 98, 107. See also 98–111.

3. Bonhoeffer, *Life Together and Prayerbook of the Bible*, 36.
4. Stephen Charles Mott, *Biblical Ethics and Social Change*, 2nd ed. (New York: Oxford University Press, 1982, 2011), 123. See his larger discussion on pages 123–142.
5. Mott, *Biblical Ethics and Social Change*, 138–141.

CHAPTER 9: NURTURE CONGREGATIONAL CULTURE
1. Scot McKnight and Laura Barringer, *A Church Called Tov: Forming a Goodness Culture That Resists Abuses of Power and Promotes Healing* (Carol Stream, IL.: Tyndale Momentum, 2020), 13–23.
2. See https://www.thesocialdilemma.com/.
3. David Brooks, *The Second Mountain: The Quest for a Moral Life* (New York: Random House, 2019), 22.
4. John Rosensteel, personal account of the transformation of New Hope Church, Portland, Oregon.
5. Carlson and Lueken, *Renovation of the Church: What Happens When a Seeker Church Discovers Spiritual Formation* (Downers Grove, IL: IVP Books, 2011), 15–16.

CHAPTER 10: RELY ON THE HOLY SPIRIT
1. Scot McKnight, *Open to the Spirit: God in Us, God with Us, God Transforming Us* (Colorado Springs, CO: WaterBrook, 2018), 79–87.

CHAPTER 11: DEPEND ON GRACE
1. Stephen Charles Mott, *Biblical Ethics and Social Change*, 2d ed. (New York: Oxford University Press, 2011), 19–32.
2. Mott, *Biblical Ethics and Social Change*, 23. Italics in the original.
3. Scot McKnight, *A Fellowship of Differents: Showing the World God's Design for Life Together* (Grand Rapids, MI: Zondervan, 2016), 38–39. Italics added.
4. James D. G. Dunn, *The Acts of the Apostles*, reprint ed. (Grand Rapids, MI: Eerdmans, 2016), 12. Italics added.
5. Beth Moore, Twitter post, August 9, 2022, https://twitter.com/BethMooreLPM/status/1557016558920163330.
6. We heard this story from editor Steve Halliday, who also helped us shape this book into its final form.

EPILOGUE: TOV IS WORTH IT
1. John Rosensteel, personal account of the transformation of New Hope Church, Portland, Oregon.
2. John Rosensteel, personal account.

ABOUT THE AUTHORS

Scot McKnight is professor of New Testament at Northern Seminary and a recognized authority on the New Testament, early Christianity, and the historical Jesus. He is the author of more than ninety books, including the award-winning *The Jesus Creed* as well as *A Church Called Tov*, *The King Jesus Gospel*, *A Fellowship of Differents*, *The Blue Parakeet*, and *Kingdom Conspiracy*. He maintains an active Substack newsletter at https://scotmcknight.substack.com. He and his wife, Kristen, live in the northwest suburbs of Chicago, where they enjoy long walks, gardening, and cooking.

Laura Barringer is a teacher and the coauthor of *A Church Called Tov*. She is also a children's ministry curriculum writer for Grow Kids and coauthored the children's version of *The Jesus Creed*. A graduate of Wheaton College, Laura resides in the northwest suburbs of Chicago with her husband, Mark, and three beagles.

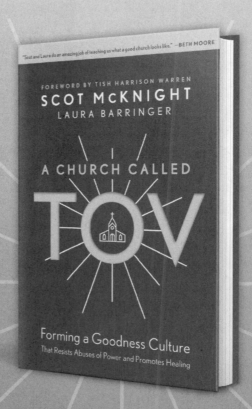